Reviews

"...I'm delighted that someone, at long last, has undertaken to write a book about this great man. *The Life and Times of Archbishop Fulton J. Sheen* is an extremely readable and straightforward biography of one of the great religious figures of the 20ᵗʰ century. Those of us who grew up listening to Bishop Sheen will find this book fascinating, and younger Catholics will catch the spirit of this great priest whose message electrified hundreds of millions of people."   —*Fr. Benedict J. Groeschel, CFR*

"Fr. Murphy's portrait of Bishop Sheen is a great gift. Written with both admiration and honesty, this book will introduce a younger generation to one of the most extraordinary Catholics of the century past, and will move their parents to recall with gratitude the extraordinary grace that was the life and priesthood of Fulton J. Sheen."   —*Rev. Richard John Neuhaus,*
Editor-in-Chief of First Things

"This is an affectionate appreciation of a man who converted many souls. Bishop Sheen's pious zeal and romantic vision have become symbols of a moment in modern Church history which for good and ill has vanished with breathtaking speed."
—*Rev. George W. Rutler*

"For more than three stormy decades, with great popular impact, Fulton Sheen proclaimed the faith and gave an understanding of the Catholic Church to Catholics and non-Catholics alike. Father Murphy captures the spirit of this remarkable pastor and teacher in showing how Archbishop Sheen was a man of deep faith who had a passion for the truth, a commitment to change people's lives and a deep devotion to the Mother of God."   —*Francis Cardinal George, Archbishop of Chicago*

"...a delight to read. Will enable a new generation to know and fall in love with the late great Archbishop Fulton J. Sheen." —*Scott Hahn*

"Father Murphy's book, *The Life and Times of Archbishop Fulton J. Sheen*, must be welcomed by all those who appreciate this great American priest's personality and mission. The author highlights powerfully the supernatural character of the Archbishop's message, whether on television or in his numerous publications, for the latter prepared his homilies on his knees in front of the tabernacle, and this gave to his words a power that the most talented human being can never reach by his own strength. That Bishop Sheen had received exceptional gifts cannot be denied, but these gifts were watered by grace, and also explain his remarkable political perceptiveness. He was one of the rare thinkers who understood how anti-Christian communism was — something that many did not perceive because of its apparent sense for social justice. Father Murphy's presentation is scholarly and objective; it is peppered with well-chosen quotations. The low ebb of Fulton Sheen's life was the three years he spent in Rochester where he experienced a sense of failure, and that God permits failure is often a grace. Archbishop Sheen had his crosses and he had his weaknesses... and yet he has been a gift to the Church. Father Murphy's book deserves to be highly commended for having enriched the tributes already paid to this remarkable cleric."
—*Alice von Hildebrand, Professor Emeritus of Philosophy, Hunter College of C.U.N.Y.*

"Your book on Archbishop Sheen is well-written as one would expect. It gives an impressive overview of the Archbishop's life. It is well-documented and clearly points out Archbishop Sheen's chief interests which were: (1) The saving of souls; (2) Devotion to the Blessed Sacrament; (3) Dedication to our Blessed Mother; and (4) Calling attention to the dangers of Communism. His major concern was for the poor. The book does not lend itself to easy quotations but, as always with Archbishop Sheen, there are memorable sentences."

—*Msgr. Florence D. Cohalan*, author of
A Popular History of the Archdiocese of New York

THE LIFE AND TIMES OF
ARCHBISHOP FULTON J. SHEEN

THE LIFE AND TIMES OF ARCHBISHOP FULTON J. SHEEN

Myles P. Murphy

ALBA·HOUSE   NEW·YORK

SOCIETY OF ST. PAUL, 2187 VICTORY BLVD., STATEN ISLAND, NEW YORK 10314

ST PAULS

Library of Congress Cataloging-in-Publication Data

Murphy, Myles P.
    The life and times of Archbishop Fulton J. Sheen / Myles P. Murphy.
      p. cm.
    Includes bibliographical references.
    ISBN 0-8189-0842-4
    1. Sheen, Fulton J. (Fulton John), 1895-1979. 2. Catholic Church—United
States—Bishops—Biography.   I. Title.

BX4705.S612M87 2000
282'.092 — dc21
[B]

                                99-087648

Produced and designed in the United States of America by the
Fathers and Brothers of the Society of St. Paul,
2187 Victory Boulevard, Staten Island, New York 10314-6603,
as part of their communications apostolate.

ISBN: 0-8189-0842-4

Printing Information:

Current Printing - first digit   1   2   3   4   5   6   7   8   9   10

Year of Current Printing - first year shown

2000   2001   2002   2003   2004   2005   2006   2007   2008   2009

Dedicated to
Jesus, the Author of Life
Mary, the Mother of All the Living
Joseph, Protector of Life

To Thomas Joseph and Margaret Mary
who gave me life, love and the greatest gift a
parent can give to their child — the treasure of
their faith.

Contents

Acknowledgments

THE THESIS THAT EVOLVED INTO THIS BOOK BEGAN THREE YEARS AGO at the International Marian Research Institute. The thesis concerned Archbishop Sheen and his Mariology or what he had to say and had written about the importance of Mary in the life of the Church and its members. One-quarter of the thesis concerned Sheen's life and times. After my defense of the thesis, the faculty at the Institute advised that I have it published. My thanks for their advice and encouragement. Thanks especially to Father Johann G. Roten, SM, Director of the Institute, for his assistance and guidance as moderator.

There is a reference used by priests given to those among their number who have had an influence upon and/or assisted one in one's priesthood. Each of the following can be described as a "priest's-priest." Thanks first to Monsignor John T. Doherty and Monsignor Charles J. McManus for proofreading both thesis and manuscript. Special thanks and appreciation, however, for their unwavering advice, support and confidence. I would be remiss if I did not mention that the gratitude expressed above pales almost into insignificance when compared with my thanks to God for introducing me to these two servants of the Lord. Their example of what priesthood is, is for me, a constant source of strength and renewal.

Thanks to Father William Graf, Archivist at the Archbishop Fulton J. Sheen Archives for his patient assistance during the course of my research at the Archives. Thanks to Mary

McLoughlin and the staff at the Society for the Propagation of the Faith in helping me locate many of the pictures used in this book. To those whom I interviewed for this book, many thanks both for your knowledge and time. Thanks to Alba House, and its director, Father Edmund C. Lane, SSP, for his assistance in the editing of the manuscript.

To my family, friends and the staff and parishioners of St. Gabriel's Parish, Riverdale, New York, who were with me every step of the way, your concern, support and best wishes, to say the least, meant so much. Finally, my gratitude and filial admiration to my bishop, John Cardinal O'Connor, Archbishop of New York, who, while in the midst of his own "Calvary," took pen and paper in hand to write the Foreword for this book.

Foreword

To be sure, the late Archbishop Fulton J. Sheen was one of the most popular preachers, personalities, and priests in the United States. Thousands upon thousands of Catholics and non-Catholics alike were inspired by his television series, *Life Is Worth Living*, radio shows, books, articles, and sermons.

The Archbishop is buried in the crypt of St. Patrick's Cathedral. I have often had cause to visit the crypt and to ponder the contribution that the Archbishop made to the Church he loved so dearly. Father Myles P. Murphy, a priest of the Archdiocese of New York, has made an important effort to capture the essence of the Archbishop's life and times.

Fr. Murphy provides us with a recounting of the Archbishop's early years and education, his extraordinary work in bringing converts to the Church, his lifelong concern for the missionary efforts of the Church, his sundry and various writings, his radio and television broadcasting efforts, his inspirational preaching ability, and most of all, his devotion to the Blessed Virgin Mary.

As Archbishop Sheen constantly reminded us, "Life is worth living." Thankfully, Fr. Murphy has provided the highlights of a life that was most worthily lived.

✠ John Cardinal O'Connor
Archbishop of New York
December 28, 1999

Introduction

H OW, THEN DO I SEE MY LIFE? I SEE IT AS A PRIEST. THAT
means that I am no longer my own but at every
moment of my existence I am acting in the person of
Christ. As a United States ambassador in a foreign
country whether at recreation or in council chambers
is always being judged as a representative of our country, so too a priest is always an ambassador of Christ.
But that is only one side of the coin. The priest is still a
man.[1]

One of the most famous and accomplished churchmen of
the last century was the late Archbishop Fulton J. Sheen. So
prevalent was the influence and popularity of Sheen in the
Roman Catholic Church, that Pope John Paul II, a son of Poland and leader of the Church, told Sheen, only two months
before his death, in front of thousands of cheering Catholics
gathered in New York's St. Patrick's Cathedral, that he had
spoken and written well of the Lord Jesus and was a loyal son
of the Church.

It was on a cold winter morning when my mother, Margaret, asked me if I would attend a wake with her in Manhat-

---

[1] Fulton J. Sheen, *Treasure in Clay*, Doubleday, Garden City, NY, 1980, p. 3. Hereaf-
ter this book will be cited as *TIC* followed by page number. The book was re-
published by Ignatius Press, San Francisco, CA in 1993.

tan. I asked, "Who died?" To which she replied, "Archbishop Sheen." I asked, "Where in Manhattan?" "St. Patrick's Cathedral," she answered. Within a few hours we were on our way into the city. While on route, my mother spoke about the man to whom we were going to pay our respects. She told me how he had been an important presence in her life and the life of my grandmother. Without fail, she and her mother would watch his program, "Life is Worth Living," each week on television. For both, it was often the highlight of the day. Over the years I had heard people speak about Fulton Sheen and I once attended Midnight Mass on Christmas Eve at St. Patrick's, where Sheen gave the homily. I asked her what it was that made him so special to her, to which she replied, "He was another Christ." Knowing that my mother was not given to exaggeration, her response always remained with me. Her answer might be a bit much for some, but it was an answer that came from the heart and the heart never lies. Somehow, Sheen had touched my mother in a way that led her to believe what she asserted. That morning the two of us waited four hours on line outside St. Patrick's with thousands of others, to view the remains of America's most famous Catholic prelate.

My next encounter with Fulton Sheen took place in the library at St. John's University. I was working on a term paper and, as anyone who has worked on a paper knows, after a time one looks for anything that will distract him/herself from the appointed task. On the table where I was working were several books. As I looked them over, I saw one entitled: *Treasure in Clay*, some of which will be quoted in the following pages. It was the autobiography of Archbishop Sheen. Putting aside my assignment, I began to read his book. Soon, I was captivated by the man and his recounting of the life that he had lived. I took the book home and read it that night. I was intrigued enough by his book to want to read not books *about* Sheen but books *by* Sheen and about the God-Man to whom Sheen had given his life. This led to my reading: *The Priest Is Not His Own* and *Those Mysterious Priests*.[2] Seven years later, at St. Patrick's Cathedral, I was ordained to the Roman Catholic priesthood.

Archbishop Sheen wrote some sixty books and dozens of articles. His books, tapes and videos continue to be of great interest to the general population and are still widely purchased some twenty years after his death. He was one of the most traveled churchmen of the century and has been compared to Jacques Maritain, G.K. Chesterton, Norman Vincent Peale and Billy Graham. Billy Graham, one of the great evangelists of modern times, called Sheen the greatest preacher of the century.

I would like to introduce the reader to the life, the times and the faith of this extraordinary man by the subject himself. Who better to tell the story of his life and faith than Fulton Sheen himself? Shortly before his death, Sheen, in his introduction to his life story, *Treasure in Clay*, stipulated that his *real* autobiography "was written twenty-one centuries ago, published and placarded in three languages, and made available to everyone in Western civilization" and "the ink used was blood, the parchment was skin, the pen was a spear." Sheen is referring to the New Testament. "The more I lift my eyes from its pages, the more I feel the need of doing my own autobiography that all might see what I want them to see. But the more I fasten my gaze upon it, the more I see that everything worthwhile in it was received as a gift from Heaven. Why then should I glory in it?" In writing his autobiography, Sheen declared that there

---

2 Sheen, *The Priest Is Not His Own*, The Catholic Book Club, London, England, 1963; *Those Mysterious Priests*, Doubleday & Co., Garden City, NY, 1974. In the preface to *Those Mysterious Priests*, Sheen states that he wrote the book for priests and laity alike, "for two persons may read a book — the one holding it in his hand, the other reading over his shoulder. As citizens are interested in 'The Making of the President,' so non-clerics may be interested in 'The Making of a Priest' though they may never be priests."

were three pairs of eyes that would read it: his own, others', and God's. It bears repeating that Sheen always saw his life as that of a priest, and that every moment of his existence he was called to be another Christ, whose autobiography, Sheen states, is the Crucifix.

Sheen wants people to realize that a priest, while given custody over Divine mysteries — is still a man. He notes in his introduction that this is why the title of his autobiography is taken from St. Paul's Second Letter to the Corinthians. St. Paul describes himself and the other apostles as being no better than "pots of earthenware" being formed by the Creator to contain the priceless treasure of His Divine Son's indwelling presence. It is what God sees that truly matters to Sheen. Concerning himself, he says:

> In the crown of thorns, I see my pride, my grasping for earthly toys in the pierced hands, my flight from shepherding care in the pierced feet, my wasted love in the pierced Heart, and my prurient desires in the flesh hanging from Him like purple rags. Almost every time I turn a page in that book, my heart weeps at what eros has done to agape, what the "I" has done to the "Thou," what the professed friend has done to the beloved.

It is hoped that in the following pages, those who already have an appreciation of the "wit and wisdom" of Fulton J. Sheen will acquire a greater awareness of the man, his beliefs and the times in which he lived. For those who will read about him for the first time, it is hoped that this book will foster within you a desire to learn more about the philosophy, theology and faith of a priest and bishop whose "diocese" was the world, and who spent his life in the service of the Gospel.

THE LIFE AND TIMES OF
ARCHBISHOP FULTON J. SHEEN

1

The Early Years

EVERY AFTERNOON ABOUT FIVE-THIRTY, WHEN I WAS STUDY-ing for the priesthood in St. Paul's Seminary, the spiritual director would give us a conference. I was paying the usual amount of attention this particular day, when suddenly I stopped listening. My mind seemed to be suffused with light. I heard not a word he uttered, but during that experience — I don't know how long it lasted — there came an illumination of soul, a light that suffused my intellect, bringing with it an overwhelming conviction of the certitude of the Faith. The Creed and the affirmation of "I believe" became not only an intellectual assent: I was momentarily possessed of the absolute and irrefutable character of Faith. As a result of that experience, I never in my life had any doubts about the Faith. My faith centered not just in the Creed, but in the Church, and it became personalized in the Pope as Head of the Church and the Vicar of Christ.[1]

Peter John Sheen was born May 8, 1895, in El Paso, Illinois, the eldest of four boys born to Newton and Julia Sheen. "Fulton," the family name of his maternal grandparents, replaced "Peter" sometime during his childhood, while he was in grade school.[2]

---

[1] *TIC*, p. 229.

[2] *Ibid.*, p. 8.

Sheen grew up in a home with a strong Catholic family tradition and was given a parochial school education. At Saint Mary's School in Peoria he soon developed into an "extremely bright pupil,"[3] and served Mass at Saint Mary's Cathedral. Sheen remembers a time when he was serving Mass at the Cathedral, assisting Bishop John L. Spalding. He was very nervous and when it came time to bring the wine and the water to the bishop, he dropped one of the cruets on the marble floor. Sheen was terrified at what he thought awaited him once Mass was over. To his surprise, after Mass, Sheen was told by the bishop: "You go home and tell your mother that I said, that, when you get big, you are to go to Louvain, and someday you will be just as I am."[4] After graduating from Saint Mary's Grammar School, Sheen attended Spalding Institute, which was operated by the Brothers of Mary. He was class valedictorian when he graduated in 1913.

For college studies, Sheen first went to Saint Viator's College and Seminary in Minnesota. At Saint Viator's, Sheen was on the debate team where he cultivated his gifts as an orator. His talents, at first, were not obvious. Father Bergin, his coach, told Sheen that he was a poor speaker, one of the worst he had ever heard. Sheen was not daunted however. After a time, success came when he realized that he should just "be natural."[5]

After receiving the B.A. and A.M. degrees from Saint Viator's, Sheen completed his seminary training at Saint Paul's. After his ordination, he attended the Catholic University of

---

[3] Reported by Ken Crotty as the recollection of a Sister of the Sacred Heart at St. Mary's School, in "Bishop Sheen's Devotion Recalled," *Boston Post*, May 9, 1953.

[4] *TIC*, p. 12.

[5] James C.G. Conniff, *The Bishop Sheen Story*, Fawcett Publications, Greenwich, CT, 1953, p. 24.

America to work towards a doctoral degree. It was there that he became committed to Thomistic philosophy and social justice with such teachers as Doctor Edward Pace and Doctor John A. Ryan, who was a leader in the field of social ethics.[6] On weekends Sheen offered Mass and preached at local churches. But he had also come to realize that he lacked a solid philosophical foundation. He confided his concerns to a faculty member who asked, "What would you like to have in education?" Sheen responded: "I should like to know two things — first, what the modern world is thinking about; second, how to answer the errors of modern philosophy in the light of the philosophy of Saint Thomas." The Professor responded: "You will not get it here, but you will get it at the University of Louvain in Belgium."[7] In September of 1921, Sheen left for Louvain along with his brother Tom who studied medicine at the same university.[8]

The University of Louvain was founded in 1425 and was suppressed in 1794 as a result of the French Revolution and accompanying wars. It was fully restored by Pope Gregory XVI in 1833, when Belgium reclaimed its independence.[9] Almost four decades before Sheen entered Louvain, a chair of Thomistic philosophy had been instituted at the request of Pope Leo XIII. Cardinal Désiré Joseph Mercier was designated to set up the Institut de Philosophie. While head of the Institut de Philosophie, Mercier established a program that was in harmony with the progress already attained in both modern science and thought. This program was based upon the encyclical of Pope

---

[6] *TIC*, p. 22.

[7] *Ibid.*, p. 23.

[8] *Ibid.*

[9] *The New Catholic Encyclopedia*, New York: McGraw Hill, 1967.

Leo XIII, *Aeterni Patris*, in which the Pope makes clear his desire for the restoration of the philosophy of St. Thomas and its application to modern times.[10] Pope Leo XIII and his great encyclical *Rerum Novarum* (1891) were to have a lasting effect on Sheen both in his studies of Saint Thomas and in his future efforts for social reform.

Sheen enrolled in the Superior Institute of Philosophy. While at Louvain, he studied metaphysics, experimental psychology, rational psychology, cosmology, modern space and time: "Everything contemporary was stressed in every area of knowledge. But along with being up-to-date, we were drenched in Aristotle, Plato and the ancients and immersed in the philosophy of Thomas Aquinas." Sheen goes on to say that, "The way the professors handled Aquinas, he did not belong to the Middle Ages; he was our contemporary."[11]

Sheen was a "devotee" of Cardinal Mercier and Dr. Leon Noel, considered to be an eminent neo-Scholastic leader at Louvain. On July 11, 1922, he received a "license in the philosophy of Saint Thomas" and emerged both a scholar and a Thomist.[12] In 1923, Sheen received a higher degree from the Louvain: *Professeur agrégé en philosophie* (equivalent to a Ph.D.), indicating that he had successfully passed the competitive examination (*concours d'agrégation*) for admission to the teaching staff of the university; such an individual was "aggregated to the faculty." Sheen had received and accepted an invitation from the faculty at Louvain to take this examination. The possible passing grades consisted of: Satisfaction, Distinction, Great Distinction and Very High Distinction. On the night of the

---

[10] "Mercier, Désiré Joseph," *New Catholic Encyclopedia*, Vol. IX, p. 671.

[11] *TIC*, pp. 24-25.

[12] *Time*, April 14, 1952, p. 74.

exam, a dinner would be served in honor of the successful candidate and induction into the faculty would take place. If one passed with Satisfaction only water would be served at the dinner; if with Distinction, beer; if with Great Distinction, wine; and with Very Highest Distinction, champagne. Champagne was served![13] It should be noted that while working towards his degree, Sheen also studied at the Sorbonne and the Angelicum College in Rome.

Three years later, in 1926, Sheen became the first American to receive the Cardinal Mercier Prize for International Philosophy at the University of Louvain. The study and importance of philosophical psychology was central in both the thinking of Mercier and in his program at the Institute. According to Sheen, Mercier looked upon "his revival of Thomistic philosophy as a solution to false science."[14] It can be deduced that both the faculty and the curriculum that Sheen was introduced to at the University precipitated his fascination with and reliance on Thomism. Sheen says as much in his autobiography when he states that he "was immersed in the philosophy of Saint Thomas"[15] and "read through every single line that Saint Thomas wrote."[16] While the writings of St. Thomas were a great influence on Sheen, he notes that his "style" was influenced by some of his contemporaries as well. Sheen does not indicate at what stage in his life all those below began to have an influence upon him but G.K. Chesterton was most certainly an early influence.

> Since my life has covered such a long span, it has undergone several influences in style. The greatest

---

[13] *TIC*, p. 28.

[14] Fulton Sheen, "Mercier and Thomism," *Commonweal* (February 10, 1926), p. 372.

[15] *TIC*, p. 25.

[16] *Ibid.*, p. 27.

influence in writing was G.K. Chesterton, who never used a useless word. At a later date came C.S. Lewis, who, with Chesterton and Belloc, became one of the leading apologists of Christianity in the contemporary world. Malcolm Muggeridge, too, has become another inspiration to me. And I must not forget poetry, particularly *The Oxford Book of Mystical Verse,* especially the poems of Stuart Kennedy and, above all, Francis Thompson. Through the years I have kept a file of favorite poems, many of which I learned by heart.[17]

After completing his studies, Sheen had to think about his future, both what to do and where to do it. He did not have long to wait before offers from both sides of the Atlantic began coming in. While working towards his degree, he had taught at Saint Edmund's College in Ware, England, so he already had some teaching experience. In 1925, Sheen received two offers, one from Nicholas Murray Butler, President of Columbia University, who requested that he start a course in scholastic philosophy there, and one from Cardinal Bourne in London, asking that, along with Father Ronald Knox, who was his colleague at Saint Edmund's, he teach theology and philosophy there.[18] Sheen did not know which offer he should accept, so he asked his bishop, Edmund Dunne. Much to his surprise the bishop told him to come home. He was assigned to Saint Patrick's parish in Peoria. After a year, Sheen was sent to Catholic Uni-

---

[17] *Ibid.,* p. 79. Malcolm Muggeridge met with Sheen shortly before the bishop died. He believed that Sheen had said a great many things, but he particularly remembered one of his statements, which he himself considered "almost a prophecy," concerning Christendom, namely: "Christendom is over, but not Christ." He also believed that Sheen was underrated as a thinker. See George J. Marlin, *The Quotable Fulton Sheen,* Doubleday, New York, 1989, p. 356.

[18] James C.G. Conniff, *The Bishop Sheen Story,* Greenwich, CT: Fawcett Publications, Inc., 1953, p. 25. Also *TIC,* p. 28.

versity of America. Sheen's bishop had already promised him, three years earlier, to Bishop Shahan at Catholic University. Sheen inquired of his bishop: "Why did you not let me go there when I returned from Europe?" The bishop replied: "Because of the success you had on the other side, I just wanted to see if you would be obedient. So, run along now, you have my blessing." Bishop Dunne recalled a somewhat different answer to Sheen's question, "I promised you to them three years ago, but everyone said you'd gotten so high-hat in Europe that you wouldn't take orders anymore. But you've been a good boy, so run along."[19] For the next twenty-four years, Sheen served on the faculty at the School of Theology at Catholic University.

Before his work at the University began, Sheen's first book was published: *God and Intelligence in Modern Philosophy.*[20] Every ten years, the University of Louvain would issue The Mercier Prize for the best dissertation in Thomistic philosophy. He received the award from Dr. Leon Noel, the new President of the Institut Superieur de Philosophe. The response that the book received resulted in Sheen's being the first American to receive the award. The book was widely acclaimed in the academic community. *America* magazine called it "an examination of what the wise men of our day think of God... in the light of the philosophy of Saint Thomas. And the examination is not merely critical and scholarly, but brilliant."[21] And in *The Month* the review was as follows:

> No book published in recent years does more credit to
> Catholic philosophy than this. It is masterly from the

[19] *TIC*, p. 42. Bishop Dunne's quote is from an article in *Time*, April 14, 1952, p. 74.

[20] *God and Intelligence in Modern Philosophy* was originally published in 1925, in both London and New York, by Longmans, Green and Co. The book was based on his dissertation for the Agrégé degree.

[21] *America*, 35 (June 19, 1926), p. 238.

first page to the last, masterly in exposition and masterly in criticism. Then again (rarest of virtues in philosophic times) it is written in a fresh, crisp style... any Catholic who knows this book and can use its treasure will be able to hold his own in the cleverest of modern company. We all owe a great debt of gratitude to Dr. Sheen for the splendid service he has done for us.[22]

The introduction to the book was written by the well-known writer and apologist, G.K. Chesterton. Chesterton believed that Sheen was a product of the prevailing atmosphere of his times, who used Thomism to illuminate modern issues. Chesterton posits that in Sheen's book, "The Catholic Church comes forward as the one and only champion of reason."[23] According to Sheen, the book was meant to apply Thomism to the modern world: "It seeks to make Saint Thomas functional, not for a school, but for a world... to suggest solutions of modern problems in the light of the philosophy of Saint Thomas."[24] Sheen felt that there was a real need for Thomas, given the "self-confessed bankruptcy of modern thought.... If solution to modern problems is a recommendation for a philosophy which, in a strict sense, is neither ancient nor modern but *ultra-moderne*, then the philosophy of St. Thomas is pre-eminently suitable to modern times."[25] According to Sheen, the thought of Saint Thomas belonged to the ages:

If need makes actuality, then Saint Thomas was never more actual than he is today. If actuality makes moder-

---

[22] *The Month*, 147 (February 1926), p. 177.

[23] Fulton Sheen, *God and Intelligence in Modern Philosophy*, Longmans, Green and Co., New York, 1925, p. vii. Introduction by G.K. Chesterton.

[24] *Ibid.*, pp. xi-xii.

[25] *Ibid.*, pp. 7-8. Sheen credits the term *ultra-moderne* to Jacques Maritain and his book *Antimoderne* (1922), p. 16.

nity, then Saint Thomas is the prince of modern philosophers. If a progressive universe is a contemporary ideal, then the philosophy of Saint Thomas is its greatest realization.[26]

Sheen was determined to advance the Catholic faith as *the* solution to contemporary problems. The Church could not be, and was not, separate from the modern world. The Church, because of its rich intellectual heritage, including Thomism, could show moderns that faith and reason are not incompatible, but because faith is both rational and intellectual, faith and reason are complementary. Sheen would fight against opponents with the ideas of Thomas, "Each succeeding day will bring to a world drunk with the anarchy of ideas, the necessity of the philosophy of Saint Thomas as the path to intellectual sobriety."[27]

---

[26] *Ibid.*, p. xii.
[27] Sheen, "Mercier and Thomism," *Commonweal* 3, February 10, 1926, p. 373.

2

Teaching

A S A PROFESSOR AT CATHOLIC UNIVERSITY, SHEEN SERVED AS AN IN-
structor of Theology and, in 1926, taught apologetics in
the School of Sacred Sciences. In 1931, he transferred to the Philosophy Department and would remain there until 1950, when
he became the National Director of the Propagation of the Faith.
Some of the courses that Sheen taught were: "Modern Idea of
God in the Light of Saint Thomas," "Modern Idea of Religion
in the Light of Saint Thomas," and "Philosophy of Science and
Religion." Those years were not without controversy. Concerns
were raised, on the part of other faculty members, that Sheen
was spending too much time on outside engagements, including public appearances and radio broadcasts. During the late
1930's and early 1940's, while teaching in the Philosophy Department, it was estimated that Sheen filled over one hundred
and fifty speaking dates a year.[1] Then there were his radio
broadcasts. During those two decades, Sheen published *Religion Without God* (1928), *The Life of All Living* (1929), and *Philosophy of Science* (1934), in addition to such popular works as:
The Divine Romance (1930), *Old Errors and New Labels* (1931),
Moods and Truths (1933), and *The Eternal Galilean* (1934). These
popular works were intended for a wider readership and were

---

[1] See "Monsignor's Tenth," *Time*, March 11, 1940.

increasingly indicative of Sheen's penchant for appealing to non-academic audiences.

Sheen was a member of the American Catholic Philosophical Association founded at the Catholic University of America in 1926. The Association's purpose was to "promote study and research in the field of philosophy, with special emphasis on scholastic philosophy."[2] In 1929 Sheen was elected secretary-treasurer, and became the president of the association in 1941.

Education would remain foremost on Sheen's agenda whether by writing, speaking or teaching in the classroom. He believed that for Catholics "education must grow out of the soil and ground of morality, religion and faith."[3] Sheen was considered to be a leading figure in the Church's Thomistic Revival and an advocate of the "primacy of the spiritual." In an address to the National Catholic Educational Association he stated:

> In these days when philosophy is not only in evolution but in revolution, and when false prophets make a religion out of their ir-religion, it behooves Catholic educators, who are charged with the responsibility of the Divine Mission, to clarify the intellectual atmosphere of our generation, expel the foul miasma of error and skepticism, and by a Christ-like charity lead men to the glorious liberty of the sons of God. It is for this purpose that we are gathered here in solemn convention, that by the corporate council of the members of Christ's Mystical Body, and the guidance of the Holy Spirit, we may be inspired to deliverance which will make for a Catholic Renaissance in the souls and hearts of men.[4]

---

[2] *Proceedings of the American Catholic Philosophical Association* 1 (1926), p. 4.
[3] Sheen, "Education in America," published in the *N.C.E.A. Bulletin* (August, 1954), pp. 50-56.
[4] Sheen, "Educating for a Catholic Renaissance", *N.C.E.A. Bulletin* XXV (August, 1929), p. 6.

As America moved from the twenties to the thirties, it found itself in the midst of an economic, political and spiritual crisis as a result of the effects of World War I and the Great Depression. Sheen believed that the Church and Thomism could play an integral role in answering and/or solving the dilemmas modern man was encountering. In *God and Intelligence in Modern Philosophy*, he states:

> If we look to the foundation, the superstructure will take care of itself. Thomistic Intellectualism is the remedy against anarchy of ideas, riot of philosophical systems, and breakdown of spiritual forces.... Intellectual restoration is the condition of economic and political restoration.[5]

Sheen was acutely aware that if Catholicism was to have any role to play in modern affairs and problem-solving it had to, on the advice of Cardinal Mercier, "always keep current."[6] According to Sheen, the Church had to realize that:

> Christian truth is the soul of our course, but secular courses are its environment. In proportion then as we vitalize the presentation of religious doctrine... we will be effective instruments in keeping national life religious, and extending the world under the glorious Kingship of Christ.[7]

The redemptive mission of the Church, after all, was to "convert the world, not condemn it."[8] Sheen stipulated that

---

[5] Sheen, *God and Intelligence in Modern Philosophy*, Longmans, Green and Co., New York, 1925, p. 8.

[6] *TIC*, p. 51.

[7] Sheen, "Educating for a Catholic Renaissance," *Op.cit.*, p.11.

[8] Sheen as quoted in the *New York Times*, February 3, 1936. Newspaper clipping files, Fulton Sheen Archives.

success could be obtained through education, enlightenment and apologetics, but not the kind of apologetics that is identified with, "apologizing, and tolerance should become identified with indifference to creed."[9] During this time the Church sought to address the pressing needs of the times through papal encyclicals and works of mercy. Fulton Sheen was one of its foremost proponents, proposing religion as a basis on which to assess contemporary times. The identification of Sheen with Thomism is affirmed by historian William M. Halsey. He refers to Sheen as "America's most successful representative of every man's Thomism," and that "from the mid-twenties to the mid-fifties Sheen's reputation passed rapidly from perhaps an American Jacques Maritain to a clerical G.K. Chesterton and then finally rested as the Catholic counterpart of Norman Vincent Peale and Billy Graham."[10]

---

[9] *Ibid.*, 35, p. 6.

[10] William Halsey, *The Survival of American Innocence*, University of Notre Dame Press, Notre Dame, Indiana, 1980, p.156.

3

Evangelist

CONVERSION BRINGS THE SOUL OUT OF EITHER CHAOS OR this false peace of mind to true peace of soul. "Peace I leave with you, my peace I give unto you. Let not your heart be troubled, nor let it be afraid" (Jn 14:27). This true peace is born of the tranquility of order, wherein the senses are subject to the reason, the reason to faith, and the whole personality to the will of God. This true peace can never come from adjustment to the world, for if the world is wicked, adjustment to wickedness makes us worse. It comes only from identification of one's own will with the Will of God.[1]

During the 1930's and 1940's, Fulton Sheen was fast becoming known throughout the country as one of the Church's best speakers and writers. This recognition was evidenced after the National Broadcasting Company offered the Catholic Church a Sunday program on national radio in 1930. Sheen already had some experience on the radio (WLWL), after giving a series of Lenten sermons at the invitation of the Paulist Fathers.[2] The Catholic Hour broadcasts on NBC radio were sponsored by the National Council of Catholic Men. Sheen was

---

[1] Sheen, *Peace of Soul*, (Liguori, MO: Liguori Publications, 1996), p. 259.

[2] *TIC*, p. 63.

chosen to give the addresses on Sundays, from 6:00 to 7:00 P.M. The program was established by the Council to expose the Catholic faith to the rest of the population and to educate the faithful. It came at a time when there was renewed anti-Catholicism because of the presidential campaign of Governor Al Smith, who was Catholic. The Council's stated objective was to use all resources to cause the Church, its doctrines and its teachings to be better known to America in order that she may be better understood in places where there is misunderstanding and prejudice.[3]

Sheen was known already as a skillful apologist and orator, so the choice was not surprising. Catholics were not the first to use radio as a means of evangelization. The first religious broadcast would take place from station WKDA in Pittsburgh on January 2, 1921. The Reverend Edwin J. Van Etton went on the air at the Calvary Episcopal Church to conduct a Vesper service. This signaled the beginning of a major push by all faiths to use the electronic media to pass on their message.

Fulton Sheen was not the first priest to be associated with radio evangelization. Father Charles Coughlin preceded Sheen and is said to have attracted the largest audience of any priest up to that time. Estimated as high as forty million, the program was described as having "a national popularity of bewildering proportions."[4] Coughlin's popularity, in comparison to Sheen's was short-lived. Father Coughlin became embroiled in controversy both with the hierarchy and the media at large and finally was silenced by Archbishop Edward P. Mooney of Detroit.

Patrick Cardinal Hayes, of the Archdiocese of New York, was the first speaker on the Catholic Hour on March 2, 1930.

---

[3] Charles A. McMahon, in "The First Year of the Catholic Hour," *N.C.W.C. Review* 13 (March, 1931), p. 9.

[4] Alan Brinkley, *Voices of Protest: Huey Long, Father Coughlin and the Great Depression*, Alfred Knopf, New York, 1982, p. 83.

The Archbishop introduced the program by stating its objective:

> This radio hour is one of service to America, which certainly will listen in interestingly and even sympathetically to the voice of the ancient Church. To voice before a vast public the Catholic Church is no light task. We feel certain that it will have both the good will and the good wishes of the great majority of our countrymen. Surely, there is no true lover of our country who does not eagerly hope for a less worldly, a less material, and a more spiritual standard among our people.[5]

The following Sunday, March 9, Fulton Sheen had his first broadcast and continued broadcasting for the next twenty-two years. His first broadcast was titled, "Man's Quest for God." In the next few years, there were so many requests for copies of his broadcasts that the N.C.C.M. and *Our Sunday Visitor*, in a joint effort, printed and distributed copies of his addresses in pamphlet form.[6] Given the wide availability, the easy distribution and low price of the pamphlets, Sheen's audience was bound to increase.[7] The relationship between Sheen and the N.C.C.M. was mutually beneficial. By 1937, the broadcast was

---

[5] An extract of Cardinal Hayes' address was printed in a pamphlet from *Our Sunday Visitor* in association with the N.C.C.M. It included a eulogy about the Cardinal by Sheen given on October 5, 1938. The pamphlet is contained in the collection of pamphlets at the Fulton Sheen Archives.

[6] See *Catholic Action*, 14 (April, 1932), p. 17. This issue includes the first notice that Sheen's addresses, and those of other speakers, would be available in pamphlet form.

[7] "With a few exceptions, almost every broadcast series reappeared as a book. From *The Divine Romance* in 1930 to *Life of Christ* in 1952. Also some of his biggest sellers were first delivered in the form of radio talks: 'Light Your Lamps' (1947), became *Communism and the Conscience of the West* published in 1948, and 'The Modern Soul in Search of God' (1947) was duplicated in *Peace of Soul* (1949)." See Kathleen Riley Fields, "Fulton J. Sheen: An American Catholic Response to the Twentieth Century" (Dissertation, Notre Dame University, South Bend, Indiana, 1989. Fields' footnote #28, p. 133).

carried over fifty-seven stations. Two thousand letters per month were being received, many of them from non-Catholics. The Executive Secretary of the National Council of Catholic Men, Edward J. Heffron, in commenting about the letters, said that they, "give hope that the lingering bitterness and misunderstanding of another day may yet be completely dissipated.... The 'Catholic Hour' is therefore serving not only the cause of religion, but the cause of democracy and education."[8]

The tenth anniversary broadcast on March 3, 1940 consisted of "Memories" of the previous ten years. Sheen believed that as a result of the hour there had been a "decrease of bigotry, but an increase of hate" (hatred not directed at him or Catholics but a kind of hostility towards God) and "a re-awakened interest in the spiritual."[9] As a result of the Depression and the beginning of the Second World War, Sheen believed that "America was never more ripe for a genuine spiritual rebirth." He seemed most proud that the Catholic Hour satisfied this need in the hearts of millions; "it never dabbled in politics; never once attacked any religion; never stirred up hatred against any person; but with scrupulous precision always had and will always have only one purpose: the salvation of souls."[10]

One result of the Catholic Hour was an increase of the number of conversions to the Catholic faith. When asked about his success in making converts, Sheen responded: "I do not make converts, Grace makes converts, and it would be blasphemy to take credit for the work God has done. Furthermore, if I kept a record of the number, I might begin to believe that I

---

[8] Excerpts of this address were printed in *Catholic Action* 19 (January, 1937).

[9] A special pamphlet was published by the N.C.C.M. and *Our Sunday Visitor* entitled "Memories: 1930-1940" (see pp. 14-15). Found in the Memorabilia Files at the Fulton Sheen Archives.

[10] *Ibid.*, p. 15.

had made them. Then I should begin to lose all my influence over souls."[11]

Sheen's ability was even recognized by secular publications of the day as responsible for many conversions. *Time*, the national news weekly, covered the tenth anniversary of the Catholic Hour with an article titled "Monsignor's Tenth." A comparison was drawn between Sheen and Father Coughlin:

> ... her (the Catholic Church's) nearest equivalent to a great preacher is the Radio-rating Father Coughlin. Last week a son of Mother Church, in whom she can take greater pride celebrated his tenth anniversary as a radio preacher. Monsignor Sheen is a persuasive, lucid speaker, with a well-cultivated voice, who can make religion sensible and attractive to great masses of people. Take away Fr. Coughlin's microphone and Social Justice and there would be little left but a parish priest. But Monsignor Sheen is much more than a pulpiteer, he is one of the Church's ablest converters.[12]

While having an effect on the Catholic faithful, Sheen was also hearing from people of other faiths. Sheen mentions, that while there were many good fruits as a result of the program, one unanticipated but much hoped for result was a noticeable growth of good will throughout the country towards Catholicism, as evidenced by his receiving many letters from Catholics, but even more letters from Jews and Protestants.[13] Sheen regretted not having kept the "hundreds of thousands" of letters that came to his office but felt obliged not to do so given the personal nature of so many of the letters he received. Bishop

[11] Gretta Palmer, "Bishop Fulton J. Sheen," *Catholic Digest*, October, 1951, p. 55.

[12] *Time*, March 11, 1940.

[13] *TIC*, p. 73.

Edwin B. Broderick, a contemporary and friend of Sheen recalls a criticism that was leveled against Sheen from some of his fellow clergy. They wondered what was the purpose of the program if it was not to convert people to the faith. A fellow priest once told him, "You keep flying over the airport but never landing."[14] But Sheen's stated purpose was not the conversion of his listeners to the Catholic faith. He insisted that the thrust of his ministry on the airwaves was not proselytizing but educating and giving witness to his faith. He nonetheless was the "most listened to American Catholic preacher of all time," who "mingled his obvious learning and scholarship with a common touch that appealed to millions."[15] In 1940, Sheen conducted the first religious service ever to be telecast.

On Sunday, March 4, 1945, Sheen celebrated his fifteenth anniversary on the Catholic Hour with an average listening audience of 4 million people in the United States alone. On that broadcast he offered to give a rosary and booklet explaining the Mysteries to anyone interested. Catholics, Protestants, and Jews were invited to join the Rosary Crusade. The Council estimated that in the next two weeks 50,000 requests were received for rosaries from every state in the Union.[16] This appeal led to numerous inquiries from a wide ranging audience about instructions in the Catholic faith. Sheen could not possibly handle all the inquiries himself but still managed to conduct classes both in New York City and Washington, D.C. His courses lasted from four to six months and consisted of eighty to one hundred hours of instruction.[17]

---

[14] Bishop Edwin B. Broderick, retired Bishop of Albany, NY, interview by author, New York City, August 7, 1999.

[15] See John Delaney's *Dictionary of American Catholic Biography*, Doubleday and Co., Garden City, New York, 1954, p. 259.

[16] John Jay Daly, "The Man Behind the Mike," *The Sign*, May 10, 1945, p. 510.

[17] *Ibid.*

4

Making Converts

A MONG THE MANY PROMINENT CONVERTS OF FULTON SHEEN, WAS the journalist/columnist Heywood Broun. William F. Buckley, noted author and journalist, recounts the conversion of Heywood Broun in his autobiography: "Upon hearing that Sheen was on the phone and wanted to speak with him, Broun picked up the receiver and asked Sheen, 'What are you calling about?' Sheen answered: 'Your immortal soul.'" Buckley notes that, "The exchange had a fairy tale ending. Broun spent some time with Monsignor Sheen and, some time later, was received into the Church." Buckley personally agreed with a warning that he came across in his readings that "No Christian, however bent on conversion, should, uninvited, approach a nonbeliever." Buckley, however, issues his own warning: "Anyone willing to take the initiative in evangelization had better be armed with the mysterious properties of a Fulton Sheen."[1]

Another two people counted among Sheen's converts were Henry Ford II, heir to the fortune of the Ford Motor Company, and Congresswoman Clare Booth Luce. *Newsweek* magazine credited him with bringing about "three of the most notable conversions of the decade," and referred to him as the "Convert Specialist."[2] The two conversions that received the

---

[1] See William F. Buckley, *Nearer, My God: An Autobiography of Faith*, Doubleday Books, New York, 1997, p. 278.

[2] *Newsweek*, February 26, 1940.

most attention however were those of Congresswoman Clare Booth Luce, and Louis F. Budenz, who was a leader in the American Communist Party. In the case of Mrs. Luce, who was also a playwright and wife of Henry Luce, editor and owner of the *Time-Life* magazine empire, it was Sheen who first initiated their meetings over dinner. Sheen recounts the story that when he began speaking about the goodness of God, she rose from her chair and said: "If God is so good, then why did he take my daughter?" Her daughter had died a short time before in a car accident. Sheen answered: "In order that through that sorrow, you might be here now starting instructions to know Christ and His Church."[3]

Sheen would meet with Louis F. Budenz over dinner as well. Budenz disliked Sheen intensely but wanted to see, at the instigation of the Central Committee of the Communist Party, if he could win Sheen over to his cause. Sheen, using Lenin and Marx, had already answered Budenz's positions in a pamphlet entitled, "Communism Answers the Questions of a Communist." Sheen told Budenz that he was not interested in talking politics but the state of his soul. The meeting ended. Six or seven years later, Budenz contacted Sheen and was later received into the faith, along with his wife and children. When recounting his initial meeting with Mr. Budenz several years earlier, Sheen reported that over dinner, he talked to Budenz about God, grace and Our Blessed Mother. Mrs. Budenz recounted to Sheen that she had asked her husband why he chose to contact Sheen, considering the animosity her husband had towards him. Her husband's reply was: "He told me that he was interested in my soul."[4]

Sheen recounts the story of a German soldier who had come to see him after World War I. During the war, the soldier

---

[3]   *TIC*, p. 264.
[4]   *Ibid.*, p. 266.

saw Catholics praying the Rosary in their foxholes. He heard
them pray it so often that he knew the prayers by heart. He
promised God that if he were to survive the war, he would
become a Catholic. In a more humorous vein, Sheen tells the
story of a well-dressed woman, with a rather affected accent
who came to see him. She explained: "I would like to become
a Catholic, but I would not want any ordinary priest to instruct
me, for I am an intellectual. Knowing your background would
you intellectualize your faith for me?" "Madam," Sheen answered, "I am willing to instruct anyone who comes to me. As
a matter of fact, a young man with leprosy who just finished
instructions sat in that very chair on which you are seated now."
With that she flew out of the house and Sheen never saw her
again.[5] According to Sheen "Kindness, Kindness, Kindness"
were the three principles for dealing with converts, for it was
"better to lose an argument than lose a soul."[6]

Father Daniel P. Noonan, who was Sheen's personal assistant for a time, recounts the story of Sheen's befriending the
eighteen-year-old Paul Scott. The story illustrates Sheen's
words put into action.

> One wet, blustery, Halloween night, he encountered
> under a street lamp a group of children in trick or treat
> costumes. Looking at him, one exclaimed, pointing at
> [Scott's] disfigured face, "He doesn't need a mask." At
> these cruel words, Scott walked away blindly into the
> darkness, numb with rage and bitterness. All this hurt
> and humiliation welled up in fury and despair. Chance
> brought him to St. Patrick's Cathedral. Though not a
> Catholic, he went in. Kneeling there, he remembered

---

[5] *Ibid.*, pp. 262-263.
[6] Sheen, "Instructing Converts: Techniques for Convert-Makers," September 1949,
Fulton Sheen Archives.

he had heard of Bishop Sheen's great work for the lepers overseas. He went to see the Bishop. "I have come to you, because I have no one else to turn to. I haven't a friend in the world." "Well, you have one now," said the Bishop. "You will never have many friends, but those you will have, will be true friends." He invited Paul Scott once a week to dinner. Because it was difficult for Paul to use his hands, the Bishop cut the meat for him. He helped him find and furnish an apartment. Paul became a Catholic. Slowly his bitterness disappeared. Yet, at times, he suffered from loneliness. "Friendship is like most things of value," the Bishop told him. "It is not easily found, but there is value even in loneliness. It will help you to appreciate the importance of friendship when it comes to you."[7]

Sheen admonished anyone with a desire to convert others to the faith to recognize that "there are only two classes of souls in the world: those who have found the faith and those who are still looking for it."[8] Those giving instruction should also appreciate that there is "some truth everywhere" and just because someone does not see things our way, "it does not make them stupid or perverse."[9] Sheen's insight into both the treatment of converts and where truth is, finds echo in *The Dogmatic Constitution on the Church:*

---

[7] D.P. Noonan, *The Passion of Fulton Sheen*, Our Sunday Visitor, Huntington, IN, 1975, p. 51. First published by Dodd, Mead, and Co., New York, 1972, p. 10. The book is considered a controversial critique of Sheen. While the book is supposed to be about Fulton Sheen, I found that the author, while dealing with the issues facing the Church, addressed them not from the perspective and beliefs of his subject, but his own. It is purely conjecture on my part, but from a careful reading of *The Passion of Fulton Sheen*, I would conclude that the rift that occurred between the two men had to do not so much with what Noonan had to say about Sheen, as with what he himself said about the Church's position on issues of the day. Father Noonan died on October 23, 1991.

[8] *TIC*, p. 266.

[9] *Ibid.*

This Church, constituted and organized as a society in this present world, subsists in the Catholic Church. Nevertheless, many elements of sanctification and of truth are found outside of its visible confines. Since these are gifts belonging to the Church of Christ, they are forces impelling towards Catholic unity.[10]

Sheen was not without his detractors. One fervent opponent was Pastor Ayer of the Calvary Baptist Church in New York. Pastor Ayer wrote an eight-page stinging attack on Sheen entitled, "Romanism's Pied Piper: A Gospel-eye view of the Roman Catholic Church's top propagandist." Ayer granted Sheen his talents but stated that Sheen had an unfair advantage in that he had, "the power of the world's most intrinsically organized institution behind him." Ayer refers to Sheen's converts as "spiritual nothings," posing the question, "To what are they converted?"

This is not Christian salvation, but a Satanic system of religion based upon the false premise of Mary's priority. This is not the faith of the New Testament. Millions of Americans are being deceived. Monsignor Sheen and the priests who labor with him are badgering and frightening a good many Protestants into the Roman fold. In reality, they are planning complete religious totalitarianism that will destroy our religious liberty, bring about collusion between Church and state, and turn America into the chaos that has blighted Europe for hundreds of years.[11]

---

[10] See "Dogmatic Constitution on the Church, Second Vatican Council" (*Lumen Gentium*), 21 November, 1964, No. 8.

[11] Ayer's pamphlet can be found in the Sheen Archives but it is undated. The pamphlet was probably written around the time of the conversions of Clare Booth Luce and Henry Ford II.

Dr. Ayer concludes his attack with a call to his audience to defend their own faith: "Until we do awake, man our ramparts and consolidate our scattered positions preparatory to a heroic stand, we may expect that Rome will go marching on." Fanny Sedgwick Colby, in an article in *The American Scholar*, asserts that many Americans were troubled by comments made by Fulton Sheen and Mrs. Luce. The "utterances of these leading Catholics are inaccurate, misleading and combustible." Miss Colby claims that it is lamentable that Catholics were being given "a platform by which they can justify intolerance and arrogance towards the sincere efforts towards good will on the part of the non-Catholic world."[12] Sheen responded to these attacks indirectly, not attacking the authors, but by making an observation such as he made in 1947 that it was "no longer Protestantism from which we must convert souls but Confucianism."[13]

Sheen would often deflect attacks upon him by telling a humorous story. One such story is as follows: "In the early days, when I was on national radio, a man came into St. Patrick's Cathedral one Monday morning and, not recognizing me, said: 'Father, I want to go to Confession. I commute from Westchester every day. I had three friends with me — all Protestants. I became very angry and spoke most disparagingly and bitterly of that young priest who is on radio, Dr. Fulton Sheen. I just cannot stand him. He drives me crazy. I am afraid that I probably scandalized those men by the way I talked about a priest. So, will you hear my confession?' I said: 'My good man, I don't think you committed a serious sin. There are moments in my life when I share exactly the same opinion about Dr. Sheen that

---

[12] *The American Scholar* 17, Winter, 1947-1948, pp. 35-44.
[13] Sheen, "Instructing Converts."

you do. Go to Communion and reserve your Confession for another day.' He left happily, saying: 'It certainly is wonderful to meet a nice priest like you.'"[14] He could also be more to the point when the need arose, as in this following observation: "There are no monuments in the world built to critics."[15]

Sheen asserted that as a result of war, insecurity, revolution and chaos, people were confused, resulting in an acceptance on the part of some, of the reality of guilt and sin, and an openness to what the Church had to offer. During the decades of the 1920's, 30's and 40's, Sheen used writing, preaching, teaching and the radio to propose the Church's position to anyone who would listen. During the next three decades, he would seek to remedy the problems of the past that were going to affect and, indeed, be the "causes" of people's support of, or fascination with, the three "ism's" of the day, namely: Communism, Nazism and Fascism. It is during this time that Sheen became the world's first televangelist.

---

[14] *TIC*, p. 298.
[15] Sheen, *Thoughts for Daily Living*, New York, Garden City Books, 1955, p. 127.

5

Whence Come Wars

WHILE MANY IN POLITICS AND THE MEDIA FOCUSED UPON THE PO-
litical, social and economic reasons for the consequences
of World War II, Sheen believed that the reasons for the war
and the ways to end it successfully, were to be found in religion and in God. Victory and the restoration of a lasting peace
would come about only as the popes had taught, through a
profound renewal of the Christian spirit. This "profound renewal of the Christian spirit" would have as its end a return to
God and salvation.[1] The goal of many Catholic leaders, including Sheen, was that American Catholics, through their support
of the war effort, would demonstrate irrevocably that Americanism and Catholicism were compatible. The problem was
that, while many agreed that there was a common enemy,
people were at odds over just which enemy was more of a
threat: Nazism, Fascism or Communism; Hitler, Franco/Mus-
solini or Stalin. There were many who took the position that
because of the Church's hierarchical structure, Catholics would
be more favorable towards the Fascists.

The Spanish Civil War, between Franco (the Loyalists or
Fascists) and the Communists, would not only divide Catholics, but all Americans, since the one who was "right" was not

---

[1] Fulton Sheen, "Peace," Catholic Hour Broadcast Series, 1942, Our Sunday Visitor, p. 10.

29

as easily distinguishable as in the case of Nazism and Communism versus Democracy. Those who believed that the Church had fascist leanings cited the Church's Concordat and Lateran Treaty with Mussolini in 1929. Sheen, who always based his opinions and instructions on Church teaching, papal encyclicals and bishops' pastoral letters, was vulnerable to these charges.[2] Indeed, many Catholics who agreed with the Church's position on Franco (during the Spanish Civil War) were "vulnerable" to charges of supporting the Fascists. While Sheen supported the idea of Concordats he nonetheless was outspoken in his condemnation of the ideology of Fascism. Sheen was well aware of the position he held as American Catholicism's chief spokesman, and so he sought to convey to Catholic and non-Catholic alike that:

> No American is interested in the distinction between the three totalitarianisms, for us they offer the same choice as between theft, burglary and larceny. I can be anti-Communist without being pro-Nazi just as I can hate caviar without being mad about limburger; but I cannot be pro-Communist or pro-Nazi or pro-Fascist without being anti-American. As Americans we are not concerned with whether a dictator has a long moustache or a short moustache, or whether he invades the soul through the myth of race or the myth of class; we are concerned only with the fact that there has been an invasion and expropriation of the inalienable liberties of man.[3]

---

[2] See Kathleen Riley Fields, "Fulton J. Sheen: An American Catholic Response to the Twentieth Century," dissertation. Notre Dame University, South Bend, Indiana, 1989, p. 150.

[3] Fulton Sheen, "Spain Through Red-Tinted Glasses," *The Irish Monthly* 67 (March, 1938), p. 38.

Comments like these were deliberate on the part of Sheen to dissuade those who had any doubts about the patriotism of Catholics. Sheen's message concerning the crisis was always based upon its religious and spiritual aspects and he advocated the notion that "democracy is a very Christian doctrine,"[4] and that the ideals of democracy could be found in the Christian tradition. Americanism would become a major part of the message that Sheen espoused both during and after the war. He held the belief that loyalty to Christ or to the Church did not mean that one could not be loyal to one's own country as well, or what he called the two greatest loyalties: the cross and the flag. However, according to Sheen, the true patriot would not hesitate to point out the failings of his country in order that they might be remedied. The true worth of every society must be measured in light of the Gospel.

In writing *The Cross and the Crisis* in 1938, Sheen anticipated that the state of the world was leading towards another crisis. Nothing had changed as a result of World War I. Irreligion remained... man had not yet returned to God and old rivalries had been replaced by new ones. There were the rise of dictatorships, both Communist and Fascist; the repercussions of the Great Depression; and the denial of the true spiritual nature of man. Sheen believed that Christendom no longer existed! Yes, Christianity still survived but had exiled itself from Catholicism. Sheen warned that, "a day is fast coming when Christians will have to unite in real Christianity to preserve it against the anti-Christian forces which would destroy it. What is all important is spiritual regeneration, for our ills will be cured by forces not involved in the crisis itself."[5] The cross, Sheen pro-

---

4 *Ibid.* See also *The Cross and the Crisis*, Milwaukee: The Bruce Publishing Co., 1938, pp. vii-viii.

5 *Ibid.*, p. viii.

posed, which is the embodiment of Christianity, was where the
world could find the solution to all its ills.

The American way of life, however, was in need of reform.
He warned that "the future of America depends on Americans'
attitude toward God and the Cross of His Divine Son."[6]
America's regeneration rested upon whether or not Americans
recognized a need for and then followed through with secur-
ing a spiritual regeneration of the country. This implied that
redemption was not only an individual matter but a social one
as well.

> Once the cross is set up again before the eyes of men
> and placed at the crossroads of civilization, as it was
> centuries ago, men will realize that redemption is so-
> cial, that we are our brothers' keepers, in helping one
> another to a fresh start, even though it is a late start.[7]

Uncertainty and confusion about the future led many
Americans to wonder just where to turn for guidance. Many
turned to the Church, and the Church utilized Sheen to get its
message across. Its message was one of reassurance in an un-
certain time, offering the Gospel to guide and give hope. Sheen
believed the Church was the only unified moral voice left on
the earth, thus more than ever, it had to be outspoken *and*
present. He used the occasion of the coronation of Pope Pius
XII, with a worldwide broadcast, to propose to the world what
the Catholic Church's mission was:

> The Church has been gradually moving out of doors,
> from a chapel to a sanctuary, and from a sanctuary to

---

[6] Sheen, *For God and Country*, P.J. Kenedy and Sons, New York, 1941, p. 73.

[7] Sheen, "The Prodigal World," Seventeen addresses delivered on the Catholic
Hour from December 29, 1951 to April 12, 1952. Washington: National Council
of Catholic Men, 1952, p. 59.

the world... the coronation of a new pontiff is the beginning of a rapprochement of the Church and the
world — a moving of the Church out of the world
through a greater comprehension of the gospel lesson
that it is the leaven of the mass, the city on a hill, the
salt of the earth, a kingdom not of this world, but for it
and its salvation.[8]

There were many at the time who were living a life consistent with the Gospel but were baffled by all that was going
on in the world. Why were these events happening? Why now,
and why are there wars? Sheen, possibly anticipating America's
entrance into the war, sought to answer these questions in his
book, *Whence Come Wars*.[9] In seeking answers to those questions, Sheen believed one must look at how God views war.
Sheen theorized that, with God, there are two reasons for war,
"War may be either something to be waged in the name of God,
or something to be undergone at the hands of God... either a
vindication of Divine Justice or a chastisement from Divine Justice."[10] The world's irreligious attitude and man's inhumanity
to his fellow man is the basis for war. Because of these, and
man's, "disturbance of the international equilibrium," "wars
may be generated out of the social order by injustice and the
forgetfulness of God."[11] Failures of the past were partially responsible for the troubles of the present. God could, Sheen reasoned, at any time stop war, but only at a terrible cost — the
destruction of human freedom. War would take a heavy toll on

---

[8] Sheen. From a reprinted copy of his radio broadcasts to mark the coronation of
Pope Pius XII, preserved in the scrapbook of "Joseph F. Sheen of Chicago," in
the Fulton Sheen Archives.

[9] Sheen, *Whence Come Wars*, Sheed and Ward, New York, 1940.

[10] *Ibid.*, p. 6.

[11] *Ibid.*, p. 5.

nations, but Sheen believed World War II was also "an opportunity for national resurrection."[12] With a return to God and the restoration of justice, peace and order could be restored. Restoration could be achieved if man was willing to accept the cross and return to justice, as outlined by the Church through the Papacy. The moral status of the Papacy and its position in the world made it uniquely the one whom the world could rely upon as the "bulwark of freedom," proposing freedom as defined by God, as opposed to the freedom defined by man, which will never come to pass.

---

[12] Sheen, "Peace," the Catholic Hour broadcast series from 1941- 1942, pamphlet by Our Sunday Visitor, Fulton Sheeen Archives, p. 19.

6

The Three Ism's

R ELIGION WAS CONSIDERED AN ENEMY BY THE THREE ISMS: NAZISM,
Fascism and Communism. Thus religions, Catholicism
and Judaism in particular, were being persecuted around the
world. This persecution was not only an offense against the
freedom of all people but an affront to God. Communism and
Fascism (of which Nazism is a form) were virtually the same.
Communism and Fascism, Sheen points out, both subscribe to
the belief that the individual exists for the state, both are intol-
erant of political opposition, hated minorities, denied freedom
of the press, were anti-religious, and hated God.[1] Sheen cautioned that the world did not have two choices, namely between
Communism and Fascism, but it had really only one choice.
Society had to realize that Communism was Soviet Fascism,[2]
and Communism is the Asiatic form of Fascism. Fascism is the
European form of Communism.[3] This was confirmed with the
1939 Nazi-Soviet Non-Aggression Pact, and lastly, Fascism
arose as a reaction against Communism.[4] The real choice, Sheen
pleaded, was between dictatorship or democracy. Sheen was

---

[1] Sheen, "Our Wounded World," Catholic Broadcast Series, Our Sunday Visitor,
    Huntington, Indiana, 1937, p. 7.
[2] Sheen, *Liberty, Equality and Fraternity*, Macmillan Company, New York, 1938, p.
    118.
[3] *Ibid.*, p. 116.
[4] *Ibid.*

outspoken in his criticism of both Fascism and Communism but believed that Communism was the greater of the two evils stating: "Communism was Soviet Fascism; Communism was Fascism gone mad."[5] Sheen considered Mussolini, Hitler and Stalin, first and foremost dictators. All three were dictators who were attempting to justify their actions by ideas which were only weapons to keep themselves in power.[6]

There was a consensus among Americans concerning the war raging in Europe, namely that Nazism and Fascism were two modern day evils that were threatening Western democracy, thus they had to be dealt with accordingly. There was no such consensus concerning the Spanish Civil War. Catholic Americans, as well as Americans in general, were divided over whom to support. Civil War broke out in Spain in 1936 with the Loyalists on one side and Communists on the other. The Church supported Franco's rebels against the Communists for two reasons: they used force against those who were destroying churches and killing priests and nuns and the rebels were against communism.[7] Some Americans who sided with Franco were accused of either supporting Fascism or taking the Red Menace too seriously, while those who supported the Communists were explaining away anti-clericalism and religious persecution. Sheen was uncomfortable with some of Franco's actions but, as mentioned earlier, saw Communism as the greatest danger to Western Civilization. He took seriously the admonition he received from Pope Pius XI, which was to "speak

---

[5] Sheen, "Our Wounded World," p. 13.

[6] Sheen, lecture given at "Loyola College" and summarized in a newspaper article preserved in the "Joseph F. Sheen of Chicago" scrapbook, Fulton Sheen Archives.

[7] Kathleen Riley Fields, "An American Catholic Response to the Twentieth Century," dissertation, Notre Dame University Press, South Bend, Indiana, p. 171.

on Communism at every opportunity, and to warn America of its dangers."[8]

The United States Government passed a "Neutrality Act" which stipulated that neither side in the Spanish Civil War could receive arms. The National Council of Catholic Men organized the "Keep the Spanish Embargo Committee," in order to publicize the position of the American Church on the Spanish Civil War. At a rally with 4,000 people in attendance, Sheen gave the keynote address. Sheen argued for support of the Act, claiming that in any civil war, "when the attack comes from inside the nation, it is not always easy to define the aggressor" and, "Let us, instead of lifting the embargo to sell gun powder to Spain, spend that money on the poor."[9] In focusing the attention of Americans on the war in Europe, Sheen hoped to have Americans concentrate on "Americanism." Sheen also wanted to respond to the opinion, held by some, that Catholics were supporting Franco and his methods. Most important to him, however, was handling what he perceived to be *the* threat to freedom around the world. In an article in the *New Republic*, Sheen is quoted thus:

> True Americanism means two things — positively, the recognition of the sovereign, inalienable rights of man, and negatively, unqualified opposition to *all* totalitarian forms — whether they be Nazi, Fascist, Communist — which deny these rights. There is irreconcilable opposition between the regimes of Russia, Germany and Italy. Over there, the state is the source of rights; here man is the source of rights. Over there, freedom

---

[8] Sheen, "Eulogies for Pope Pius XI," p. 13.

[9] The addresses given at the rally were published by the N.C.C.M. Sheen's addresses can be found at the Fulton Sheen Archives. Many years later, Sheen made a similar statement in a call for an end to the Vietnam War. See p. 95 of this book.

resides in the collectivity: in the race as in Germany, in the nation as in Italy, and in the class as in Russia; over here, freedom resides in man.[10]

An example of those who were suspicious of the loyalties of the Church and Sheen (as to whether the Church and Sheen looked favorably upon Democratic or Fascist ideals), can be found in a letter written by Ernest Sutherland Bates titled, "An Open Letter to Monsignor Fulton J. Sheen." The letter was published in *New Republic* magazine. Bates had been an admirer of Sheen but now questioned Sheen's loyalty because of his support of the Neutrality Act. Bates charged that neutrality was a "cheap evasion" and charged that Sheen and other American Catholics were "hypocrites and liars."[11] Sheen, following past practice, did not defend himself directly against the charge. Michael Williams, however, responded in an article in *Commonweal* magazine, defending both Sheen and American Catholics.

> Reasonable Catholics would not and do not say that American liberals who support the Loyalists are all allied with the Communists and Anarchists, and at heart are dishonest in their lip service of democracy and religious liberty. Charges of that character are usually explosions of emotion, excusable of course, but not helpful to a discussion in which reason should control even righteous emotions.[12]

---

[10] Address given by Sheen at the rally sponsored by the N.C.C.M. for the passage of the "Neutrality Act." Pamphlet found at the Fulton Sheen Archives, pp. 37-38.

[11] Ernest Sutherland Bates, *New Republic* (February 1, 1939), pp. 371-372. Ironically, Mr. Bates, when reviewing Sheen's *God and Intelligence in Modern Philosophy* said that the book was "one of the most important contributions to philosophy that has appeared in the present century." See *Commonweal* 3 (July 13, 1926), pp. 254-265.

[12] *Commonweal* 30, February 10, 1939, p. 436.

However, in an interview after the war, Sheen explained his position, "I never defended Franco. I always defended Spain against the attack of the Communists. Simply because one is anti-Communist, it does not follow that he is a Fascist. Franco was the lesser of two evils."[13] Sheen insisted that while there was no Fascist threat in the United States, there was a Communist one. Thus the threat of Communism had to be dealt with, warning that "the struggle is between Communism and anti-Communism."[14] Sheen's underlying motive throughout these crises years was the defense of freedom of religion and from religious persecution. Sheen believed that the main threat to freedom of religion, as well as other freedoms, was Communism. In the following decades, Sheen would use all his talents both to inform and persuade the public that the danger to the world would come out of Russia, not so much because of its strength as because of our weakness:

> Our modern crisis is born of the fact that there has been a great divorce, a divorce between those who have the Truth and those that have the zeal or the fire. The Western world possesses the Truth in its highest manifestations; the Communist world has not the Truth, but it has the fire, heat, energy, zeal, love of sacrifice, dynamism. Our Western world has the light, but no heat; the Communists have the heat but no light. If we who have the truth were anxious to communicate it, there would be love — love enough to die for it. If Truth and love were ever united, the world would be at peace. The present problem is this: will the Communists, with all the fire and zeal and intention, recover the Truth

---

[13] Kenneth Stewart, "An Interview with America's Outstanding Roman Catholic Proselytizer," *P.M. Magazine*, June 16, 1946. A copy can be found at the Sheen Archives.

[14] Sheen, "The Tactics of Communism," *Sign* 16, November, 1936, pp. 201-204.

before those who have the Truth become aflame with love for it? It is our guess that the Communist world will find the Truth. When Russia discovers the Faith, it will sweep it throughout the entire Western world; then we will know that Christianity has not failed.[15]

---

[15] Sheen, *The Church, Communism and Democracy*, Dell Publishing Company, New York, 1954, p. 12.

7

Communism: The Threat

S HEEN WAS IN AGREEMENT WITH THE SENTIMENTS OF POPE PIUS XI, and his belief that Communism was a threat that had to be addressed. The Holy Father said:

> This all too imminent danger is Bolshevistic and Athe-
> istic Communism which aims at upsetting the social
> order and at undermining the very foundation of
> Christian civilization. In the face of such a threat, the
> Catholic Church could not and does not remain silent.[1]

While suspicious of Fascism and the alliance between Hitler and Stalin, Sheen believed that, in the long run, the threat to Democracy and Europe would come from Russia. He warned:

> Look out for Russia that walks like a bear and crawls
> like a snake. Mark these words: the enemy of the world
> in the near future is going to be Russia, which is play-
> ing democracies against dictators, which is using peace
> when it can and war when it must, and is preparing,
> when Europe is exhausted from war, to sweep over it
> like a vulture to drink its blood and make away with
> the spoils.[2]

---

[1] Pope Pius XI, "Divini Redemptoris" (1937). *The Papal Encyclicals*, McGrath Publishing Co., A Consortium Book, Wilmington, NC, 1981.

[2] Sheen, *War and Guilt*. Nineteen addresses of the Catholic Hour from December
15, 1940 to April 13, 1941. Washington: National Council of Catholic Men, 1941.

After Hitler broke with Russia and invaded her, an alliance between the Allies and Russia was of great concern to Sheen because of its moral inconsistency. Sheen equated Stalin and Hitler as forces of evil and compared them to "Pilate and Herod, (who were) Christ haters."[3] He pointed out that after we helped the Russians, they allied themselves with Hitler in the Nazi-Soviet Non-Aggression Pact. Then, when Hitler invaded Russia, we assisted Stalin again. Sheen complained that because of political expediency, countries were willing to enter into pacts with the devil: "Nations which boast that they are defending religion seek to enter into pacts with anti-religious governments."[4] Indeed, Sheen's prophecy came true once the war had ended. In his autobiography, Sheen relates that, "Just before World War II when Russia and Germany were still enemies, I made the prophecy on radio that as 'Pilate and Herod were enemies and became friends over the bleeding body of Christ, so one day Communism and Nazism, which are now enemies, will become friends over the bleeding body of Poland.'[5] The prophecy came true as the Nazis and Soviets were united." The longtime foe of Stalin and Communism was not surprised that Stalin would turn his attention to Eastern Europe, for he had warned in 1939:

> Russia had finally succeeded in turning Europe into a battlefield... the danger to civilization is not a result of the war between Hitler and the Allies. It will be the consequence of that war, when Communism will

---

[3] Sheen, "The Seven Last Words and the Seven Virtues," Seven addresses of the Catholic Hour from February 11 to March 24, 1940. Washington: National Council of Catholic Men, 1940. *The Seven Last Words* was published by Garden City Books in 1952 and by Alba House in 1996.

[4] Sheen, *Whence Come Wars*, Sheed and Ward, NY, 1940, p. 4.

[5] *TIC*, p. 88.

sweep over Europe. Then the war shall not be between nations, but between philosophies of life.[6]

After the breakdown of the alliance following the war, America realized that Russia was indeed a threat, something that both the Church and Sheen had been saying for years. Sheen continued to do what he had already been doing for nearly twenty years in his books, articles and sermons, warning against Communism, this "complete philosophy"[7] and "philosophy of life which mobilizes souls for economic and secular ends."[8] Sheen's position would be based upon not only his own lifelong study of Communism[9] but upon the writings of the popes: Pope Pius XI and his encyclicals, *Atheistic Communism, Divini Redemptoris* (*On the Divine Redeemer*) and *Mit brennender Sorge* (*With Bitter Sorrow*), as well as Pope Pius XII's *The Mystical Body of Christ*. Sheen a "prophet and philosopher"[10] of the dangers of Communism would spend the rest of his life fighting this threat which he believed to be the greatest threat to religion since ancient Rome. Bearing in mind the words of Jesus to "love the sinner, but hate the sin," while underscoring his love for Russia,[11] Sheen insisted on loving the communist but hating Communism, emphasizing that "the truly Catholic attitude toward Russia must not be such that it will condemn the sinner so as to prevent his conversion."[12]

---

[6] Sheen, "Moscow Makes Confusion for Reds and for Other Nations," *America*, October 28, 1939, p. 61.

[7] *TIC*, p. 81.

[8] Sheen, "The Mystical Body, or The Church and Communism," copy of Sheen's lecture, at the Sheen Archives, p. 16.

[9] *Ibid.*, p. 88.

[10] Donald F. Crosby, S.J., *God, Church and the Flag: Senator Joseph R. McCarthy and the Catholic Church, 1950-1957,* The University of North Carolina Press, Chapel Hill, NC, 1978, p. 15.

[11] *TIC*, p. 89.

[12] Sheen, "Soviet Russia May Be Helped, But Russia Must Be Reformed," *America* 65, October, 1941, p. 35.

Ultimately, Sheen believed that Russia would return to Christianity. His belief was based upon the apparitions of the Blessed Virgin Mary to three children (Lucia, Jacinta, and Francisco) in Fatima, Portugal, in 1917. As with Lourdes, Sheen made many pilgrimages to Fatima, which, like Lourdes, is one of the major Marian shrines in the world. During one of her six apparitions, on the thirteenth of the month, from May to October of 1917, Mary told the three seers:

> ... in the end my Immaculate Heart will triumph. The Holy Father will consecrate Russia to my Immaculate Heart, Russia will be converted and an era of peace will be given to the world.[13]

Sheen described the apparitions and warnings during one of his radio broadcasts. To those who were less than enthusiastic about Fatima, Sheen's response was: "We are not concerned about proving the authenticity of these phenomena at Fatima, for those who believe in the realm of the Spirit and the Mother of God need no proof, and those who reject the Spirit would not accept it anyway."[14] Sheen adhered to the admonition of Pope Pius XI, as mentioned earlier, that he should alert America to the dangers of Communism,[15] by publishing *The Cross and the Crisis*,[16] *Liberty, Equality and Fraternity* both in 1938[17]

---

[13] Sheen, *Communism and the Conscience of the West*, Garden City Books, Garden City, NY, 1948, p. 204. The Cause for the Canonization of Jacinta and Francisco has been introduced.

[14] Thomas A. Ksekman and Steven Avella. "Marian Piety and the Cold War in the United States," *Catholic Historical Review*, LXIII. July, 1986, pp. 403-424.

[15] Daniel Noonan, *The Passion of Fulton Sheen*, Our Sunday Visitor, Huntington, Indiana. 1975, p. 51. First published by Dodd, Mead, and Co., NY, 1972.

[16] Sheen, *The Cross and the Crisis*, The Bruce Publishing Co., Milwaukee, WI, 1938.

[17] Sheen, *Liberty, Equality and Fraternity*, Macmillan Company, NY, 1938.

and *Communism and the Conscience of the West* in 1948.[18] In *Communism and the Conscience of the West*, Sheen asserts that:

> As Western civilization loses its Christianity, it loses its superiority. The ideology of Communism rose out of the secularized remnants of a Western Civilization whose soul was once Christian. Communism is, therefore, as Waldemar Gurian has said, both an "effect and a judgment on the Western world."[19]

When Japan attacked Pearl Harbor, America's entry into the war against the Axis powers was assured. Sheen believed that America's entry into the war was justified because its entry met the criteria of the "Just War."[20] Sheen had three criteria for a just war: "A morally good end, right intentions, and justifiable methods." Because of the war, America would not be spared the cross, but Sheen believed if she accepted the cross and carried it well, there was promise for the future. Sheen continued to maintain that war was a judgment from God and that World War II came about for the same reasons as the First World War, namely, secularism or irreligion and lack of charity. Sheen believed that man had not as yet turned from the apostasy (a false way of life) that caused World War I. This con-

---

[18] Sheen, *Communism and the Conscience of the West*, Bobbs, Merrill Co., Indianapolis, IN, 1948. According to Bernard Iddings Bell in his article, "Faith versus the Economic Animal," published in the *New York Times Book Review* in April 1948, Sheen "shows here a development into something of the stature of a prophet." Michael D. Reagan in a review of the book says that Sheen "presents a vital message in disclosing the essential religious character of the fix that the world was in. With a force that cannot be ignored he stresses our share in the growth of atheistic communism. He has given us a message that must be heeded: God will be served or man will perish." *America*, Vol. 79:8, April 10, 1948.

[19] *Ibid.*, p. 8.

[20] Sheen, *War and Guilt*, Nineteen addresses of the Catholic Hour from December 15, 1940 to April 13, 1941. Washington: National Council of Catholic Men, 1941, p. 137.

tinued apostasy resulted in a new World War.[21] However, this war, like World War I, could "unmask a false way of life and shatter secular illusions."[22] Sheen explained to his audiences that God permits evil from time to time for the sake of a greater good.[23] Sheen proposed that peace with justice could be achieved after the war if the world followed the Five Point Peace Plan of Pope Pius XII. He stressed that while these guidelines were proposed by the head of the Catholic Church, and not the head of a democratic nation, the points were in accord with all the principles of democracy.[24]

The Five Point Peace Plan is as follows: (1) assure all nations of their right to life and independence, (2) release nations from the slavery imposed upon them by the race for armaments, (3) erect some juridical institution which shall guarantee the loyal and faithful fulfillment of treaties, (4) establish strictly legal rights for the real needs and just demands of nations, populations and racial minorities, (5) restore deep and keen responsibilities which measure and weigh human statutes according to the sacred and inviolable standards of the laws of God.

Sheen counseled America that she could win the war if our goal was in accord with that of the Creator and if people realized that the war was not only about freedom... the war was also a theological struggle between Totalitarianism, Secularism and Christianity. While the Western World was fighting

---

[21] Sheen, *The Crisis in Christendom*. Eighteen addresses of the Catholic Hour, from January 3 to April 25, 1943. Washington: National Council of Catholic Men, 1943, p. 2.

[22] Sheen, *War and Guilt*. Nineteen addresses of the Catholic Hour from December 15, 1940 to April 13, 1941. Washington: National Council of Catholic Men, 1941. Sheen's purpose was to give the theologian's view of war rather than the journalist's.

[23] *Ibid.*, p. 114.

[24] Sheen, *War and Guilt*, p. 54.

threats to democracy from without, the Western World had to change within. God would support our efforts, if we were truly serious about living up to our Judeo-Christian tradition. Yes, we must fight against the Axis powers, but we must also fight against a barbarism from within. The American Bishops spoke along these same lines in their pastoral letter *The Essentials of a Good Peace*:

> Let us make ourselves in truth peacemakers.... Let us recognize the problems in our own social life and courageously seek the solution of them. A first principle must be the recognition of the sovereignty of God and of the moral law in our national life, and in the right ordering of a new world born of the sacrifices and hardship of war.[25]

During these worldwide years of crisis, Sheen played a role in both educating Catholics and all Americans about the dangers from without and within. He differed from many others in that he saw present ills from a theological vantage point. He agreed with the American Bishops:

> Secularism, or the practical exclusion of God from human thinking and living, is at the root of the world's travail today. It was the fertile soil in which such monstrosities as Fascism, Nazism, and Communism could germinate and grow. It is doing more than anything else to blight our heritage of Christian culture, which integrates the various aspects of human life and renders to God the things that are God's. The ideals of Christianity have never been fully realized just as the

---

[25] Hugh Noonan, *The Pastoral Letters of the American Hierarchy, 1792-1970*, United States Catholic Conference, Washington, DC. "The Essentials of a Good Peace," in *Pastoral Letters* (Vol. II), p. 49.

ideals of the Declaration of Independence and our Constitution have never been fully realized in American political life.[26]

When man loses sight of God and seeks answers to all the problems of life through his own abilities, and without God, he loses his way and crises originate.[27] While it is true that Sheen used his abilities to further the message of the Gospel and the Church, he also championed democracy and freedom. He wanted to demonstrate that loyal Catholics could be loyal Americans as well, and that democracy and Catholicism could co-exist because both emphasized the rights and dignity of man. Neither, however, could co-exist with enemies of democracy and religion. Therefore, he pleaded for the unity of "all men of good will — Jews, Protestants, and Catholic alike" — in resisting Communism.[28]

On Labor Day, 1955, Sheen became the first Latin Rite Bishop in history to offer a Solemn Byzantine Rite Mass in English. More than 150,000 people joined him in Uniontown, Pennsylvania to pray for "Holy Russia," and the event was beamed abroad by the Voice of America. Sheen while remaining a fervent foe of Communism for the remaining decades of his life, made a prophetic statement in 1954 that has partially come true:

> From a material point of view, it is likely that the United States will continue to be the great world power for some decades. From a spiritual point of view, and this is the only point of view that really matters, the future

---

[26] *Ibid.*, "Statement on Secularism," in *Pastoral Letters* (Vol. II), p. 74.

[27] *Ibid.*, p. 119.

[28] Sheen, *Communism and the Conscience of the West*, Bobbs, Merrill Co., Indianapolis, IN, 1948, p. 46.

does not belong either to Western civilization, as it presently exists, or to Soviet Russia. But it is our belief that, in the decades to come, Russia, after throwing off Communism, will become the spiritual leader of the world.[29]

[29] Sheen, *The Church, Communism and Democracy*, Dell Publishing Co., NY, 1954, p. 57.

8

Televangelist

Y OU CAN GENERALLY TELL A MAN WHO HAS A TELEPROMPT-
er because he dares not take his eyes off it.... I've
always been afraid to use one. I heard once of a politi-
cian who was giving a speech and he said, "All of us
are grateful to that great man who fought so valiantly
at Valley Forge, who crossed the waters of the Dela-
ware... who became the first president of the United
States." And the thing got stuck and to this day he
doesn't know the next line.[1]

During the 1950's, Sheen received many awards, includ-
ing the New York American Legion's gold medal for his "work
on behalf of Americanism," and Notre Dame's annual Patriot
Award.[2] He also received the Marian Library Medal from the
University of Dayton, Ohio, and the Cardinal Gibbons Award,
from the Alumni Association of the Catholic University of
America for "distinguished and meritorious service to the
Church, the United States and the Catholic University."[3] These

---

1 Sheen, "Macbeth."
2 Kathleen Riley Fields, "An American Catholic Response to the Twentieth Century," dissertation, Notre Dame University Press, South Bend, IN, p. 314.
3 Jasper Green Pennington, "Fulton John Sheen: A Chronology and Bibliography,"
   Essays In Honor of Joseph P. Brennan, Saint Bernard's Seminary, Rochester, NY, 1976,
   p. 110.

awards both were a result of and contributed to the popularity of Sheen. Sheen would now not only be heard from the pulpit and on the radio, but through a medium that would be *the* catalyst in enhancing Sheen's position in the Church and throughout the country. His popular television series was originally titled "Is Life Worth Living?", but Sheen changed it to "Life is Worth Living." The program aired from 1951-57.[4]

In 1952, Sheen received an Emmy. He was awarded the Look Television Award for three consecutive years. After hearing Bob Hope thank his writers upon receiving his Emmy, Sheen upon receiving his, thanked his: "I want to thank my writers too — Matthew, Mark, Luke and John." Though those who tuned in to his show found Sheen always dressed in a bishop's traditional garb, his lectures were addressed to an ecumenical audience while remaining essentially Catholic.[5] In 1952, according to the American Research Institute, the "audience rating" for Sheen's program was 23.7, the highest ever recorded for anyone on TV during those early days of television. The bureau estimates that Sheen's program was watched by 5.7 million people weekly. His office received thirty thousand letters in one delivery with an average of from eight to ten thousand letters per day. When asked once why his television show was so popular, Sheen explained that "The Lord once used an ass to ride into Jerusalem. Now He uses an ass on TV." Sheen once quipped that he went on television to assist his sponsor — the Lord!

Actually, Sheen's program was sponsored at first by the

---

[4] *Ibid.*, p. 126.

[5] Jack Gould, in reviewing the show for *The New York Times*, said that "while Bishop Sheen's point of view reflects the doctrine of the Catholic Church, he is not using television for proselytizing or sectarian ends. A member of the Protestant or Jewish faiths can draw strength and inspiration from his words just as easily as a Catholic." See Gould, *New York Times*, February 27, 1952.

DuMont Network and its producer was a New York diocesan priest — Father Edwin B. Broderick, then at the offices of the Confraternity for Christian Doctrine and appointed first Director of Radio and Television, and later appointed Bishop of Albany. Sheen and Broderick, who lived at the priests' residence at St. Patrick's Cathedral, would occasionally have breakfast at the Cathedral residence when Sheen visited. Broderick asked Sheen what he would do if he had a television program. Sheen responded that he would give instruction about the Catholic faith. Father Broderick approached James Caddigan, program director at DuMont, with an idea for a religious program hosted by Sheen. It just so happened that at the time, the DuMont Network was looking for someone to host a show on their network opposite Milton Berle's *Texaco Comedy Hour* which aired on Tuesday nights. Such was the success of Berle's show that any show that was on at that time on another station was considered on the "Obit. Spot," or dead time. At the time, DuMont was airing old movies. As mentioned earlier, Sheen was already widely known because of his radio program and his writings. Caddigan was aware of Sheen's sucess and agreed that a program hosted by Sheen on DuMont would be fine. Father Broderick pitched the whole idea to Francis Cardinal Spellman, then Archbishop of New York. Spellman thought that a program with Sheen as its host was a good one. Sheen was approached by Broderick and agreed. But DuMont and Sheen had different ideas about the program. Sheen envisioned a program emanating from different churches in New York while giving instruction about the Catholic faith and taking questions from the audience. The studio envisioned the telecast taking place in a studio, which would keep costs down, having an audience but no questions. Caddigan was afraid that, during a live telecast, someone in the audience could cause a commotion or embarrass the Bishop and the Church. Sheen relented and agreed to the format. And so Sheen's program was telecast from the Adelphi Theatre on West Fifty-Fourth Street.[6]

The show was originally broadcast on three television stations: Chicago, New York and Washington. Within a week the network had received 3,000 fan letters and ratings for CBS and NBC dropped. Because of the popularity of the show, Admiral Television offered to sponsor the show on ABC and on more stations, with a weekly salary paid to Sheen. Sheen gave his salary to the Missions. The show continued on Tuesdays, in what was also referred to in the television industry as a "commercial burial ground."[7] What was thought would never happen, happened, with *Life is Worth Living* beating Milton Berle's *Texaco Comedy Hour* in the ratings. Up until the airing of *Life is Worth Living, The Texaco Comedy Hour* was the most popular television show in America. Milton Berle (Uncle Milty) once quipped he didn't mind losing viewers to "Uncle Fulty." Berle remarked, "If I am going to be eased off TV by anyone, it's better that I lose to the one for Whom Bishop Sheen is speaking."[8]

Sheen needed hardly any assistance while in the studio. Most television "stars" at that time made use of Teleprompters or idiot cards, as well as many writers, an orchestra and/or background music — and their programs were pre-recorded. Sheen's *Life is Worth Living* was broadcast live. Several writers would write jokes for the stars. Sheen wrote his own lines and jokes and had no rehearsals. Yet, he held onto huge audiences weekly and eventually was telecast on ninety-eight stations throughout the United States and Canada.

Sheen was also popular with members of the entertain-

---

[6] Bishop Broderick interview.

[7] Charles A. Morris, *American Catholic: The Saints and Sinners Who Built America's Most Powerful Church*, Random House, Inc., NY, 1997, p. 225.

[8] Christopher O. Lynch, *Selling Catholicism*, University Press of Kentucky, Lexington, KY, 1998, p. 8.

ment industry. Some would visit his set to pick up a few point-
ers. Jackie Gleason, one of the giants of television folklore, was
a friend of Sheen's and would visit the set on Tuesday nights.
He was in awe of Sheen's timing, poise and manner of delivery.[9] The story goes that Sheen flew to Florida for a birthday
party for Gleason where he was asked to pay tribute to his
friend. The June Taylor dancers were there to perform as well.
A TV cameraman was there and noticed the dancers passing
by Sheen. The man inquired, "Your Excellency, aren't you em-
barrassed to be among all these pretty dancers?" Sheen smiled
broadly and quipped. "No, even though I am on a diet, I can
still look at the menu."

Another famous television star at the time was Ed Sullivan. Though it cannot be said that they were close friends, upon
hearing that Sullivan underwent a serious operation, Sheen
went to visit him at the hospital. Sullivan's wife who was Jewish, believed that it was Sheen's visit that was a turning point
in her husband's recovery.

Though Sheen was a competitor of Milton Berle's, both
were very good friends. Both appeared on a Mike Douglas talk
show together where Douglas asked Sheen if he was camera
shy. Before Sheen could answer, Berle blurted out, "Camera
shy? — why he is a bigger ham than I was." Berle also claimed
that Sheen arrived at a benefit they were attending in a Rolls
Royce — with stained-glass windows. He was just one of many
celebrities who attended Sheen's funeral.[10]

Loretta Young, star of stage and screen, was a big fan of
Sheen's and believed he was the greatest orator of his time.
There is the story that Loretta Young was upset when she
learned that Sheen was no longer going to give the series of

---

[9] Bishop Broderick interview.
[10] D.P. Noonan, *The Passion of Fulton Sheen*, passim.

Lenten sermons at St Patrick's Cathedral. Her secretary called and asked to meet with Cardinal Spellman's secretary, Edwin B. Broderick, who was a Monsignor at the time, to discuss the situation. Monsignor Broderick met with Young's secretary and said he would bring the matter to the attention of Cardinal Spellman. When Broderick broached the subject with the Cardinal, Spellman said he didn't know anything about it and that he should go and talk to the Rector of the Cathedral, Auxiliary Bishop Joseph Flannelly. Broderick was concerned; after all, he was going to be putting a bishop on the spot. Spellman told him to say that, at the Cardinal's suggestion, he was asking what the story was. When Broderick met with Bishop Flannelly, Flannelly stated that he just wanted some variety and not the same speaker every year. At a later date Sheen was back at the Cathedral. It has been thought it was Cardinal Spellman who was responsible for Sheen no longer giving the Lenten Series at the Cathedral when in actuality it was Spellman who brought him back.[11]

Pearl Bailey, the great singer and humanitarian, ten years after Sheen's death remarked that, "In our lifetime we will not forget Fulton Sheen. His words will be forever; his messages touch the mind and the heart. Few men have that quality. Only love can supply that."[12]

Sheen loved art, and even though his own artistic skills were poor (he claimed a viewer once offered to provide him with classes for free at an Art School), he counted the world famous portrait artist Yousuf Karsh and the painter Salvador Dali among his friends. Karsh did the photographic work on four of Sheen's most successful works: *These Are the Sacraments*,

---

[11] Bishop Broderick interview.
[12] George J. Marlin, *The Quotable Fulton Sheen*, Doubleday, NY, 1989, p. 356.

This Is the Mass, This Is the Holy Land, and *This is Rome.* And Sheen used Dali's painting of "Christ of St. John of the Cross" as the cover for his best-selling work, *Life of Christ.*[13]

Such was Sheen's success that James Conniff wrote in his book, *The Bishop Sheen Story,* that Sheen was "preaching to more Protestants than any other priest ever has," and "there can hardly be any question that the most influential voice in Christendom, next to that of Pope Pius XII, is being raised inside a TV tube by a 58-year-old ex-farm boy from Peoria."[14] Within a year of appearing on television Sheen made the cover of *Time* magazine and was described as "perhaps the most famous preacher in the United States, certainly America's best known Roman Catholic priest and the newest star of television."[15]

Toward the end of his life, his reputation well established, he made a truly memorable TV appearance on Robert Schuller's famous *Hour of Power,* further solidifying his well-deserved reputation as an ecumenist and master televangelist. This segment has been rebroadcast several times since to the edification of a whole new generation of viewers.

---

[13] D.P. Noonan, *The Passion of Fulton Sheen,* p. 94.

[14] James C.G. Conniff, *The Bishop Sheen Story,* Fawcett Publications, Greenwich, CT, 1953, p. 5, 1, respectively.

[15] *Time,* April 14, 1952, p. 72.

9

The Popes and Sheen

I HAD SUCH REVERENCE FOR THE VICARS OF CHRIST because I saw in them the visible head of the Body of Christ, the Church. It always grieved me to see little candles spluttering in contempt at the corporate and garnered wisdom of the Church. The self-conquest of the ascetics, the endurance of her martyrs, the holiness of all the long line of Pontiffs, except a few, both exalted and abashed me. As I saw how each Pontiff respected the Scripture, tradition and the Magisterium of the Church, it was to me a kind of a trinity through which the Word of God reached us; and I realized what a joy it was not only to think "with the Church," but "in the Church."[1]

Every year Sheen received a private audience with Pope Pius XII, and this practice continued under Popes John XXIII and Paul VI. At one of those audiences, Pius XII told Sheen he was a "prophet of the times." Both Pius XII and John XXIII told him that he would have a high place in heaven. Sheen commented that "Nothing that he (Pius XII) said was infallible, of course, but his words gave me much consolation." John XXIII made his remarks to Sheen after letting him know that he was aware that he had suffered much. He invited Sheen to visit his

---

[1] *TIC*, pp. 248-249.

family in northern Italy and asked Sheen if there was anything that he could do for him, to which Sheen responded that he only wanted to do the will of God. The Pope responded: "That makes it very easy for me." "From all eternity," continued the Pope, "God knew that I would be Pope; you would think that he would have given me a better body!" At the end of another audience, the Pope asked Sheen to take a picture with him, "Come let us have our picture taken. It may make some in the Church jealous, but that will be fun." One evening, Sheen received a phone call that the Pope would like to see him. At first, Sheen thought it was a joke. But on arrival, a Swiss guard said: "Hurry up! His Holiness wants to see you." As Sheen was brought in to meet him, the Pope said: "I hope that I did not disturb you at this hour! But I just wanted to give you a gift." The Pope presented Sheen with a topaz episcopal ring and a pectoral cross saying: "Now put them in your pocket and hide them for a moment. I do not want to make other bishops envious."[2]

Sheen met annually as well with Pope Paul VI who succeeded John XXIII. During the pontificate of Paul VI there was much tribulation and difficulty as a result of the implementation of the directives of the Second Vatican Council. Sheen was not surprised at the tensions that developed after the Council:

> It is an historical fact that whenever there is an outpouring of the Holy Spirit, as in a General Council of the Church, there is always an extra show of force by the anti-spirit or the demonic. Even at the beginning, immediately after Pentecost and the descent of the Spirit upon the Apostles, there began a persecution and the murder of Stephen. If a General Council did not provoke the spirit of turbulence, one might almost doubt

---

2   *Ibid.*, passim, p. 232.

the operation of the Third Person of the Trinity over the Assembly.[3]

At an audience with Pope Paul VI, the Pope reflected on suffering and what St. Paul had said in the Letter to the Colossians namely, "we fill up the quota that is wanting in the sufferings of Christ for the sake of His Body, the Church." The Pope then took a blank piece of paper and wrote: *nolo sine cruce crucifixum* (I do not wish to be crucified without a cross). Sheen had the piece of paper framed and placed above his bed. Paul mentioned to Sheen that every night, when he went to bed and placed his head on his pillow, he really laid it on the crown of thorns. His suffering, however, brought him great joy because he believed that he was suffering for the Church.[4]

Sheen did not know Pope John Paul I who was pope for only thirty-three days but he met Pope John Paul II when he visited New York in 1979. Sheen narrated his visit to the United States on national television as he did during Pope Paul VI's visit. Sheen greeted Pope John Paul II in the sanctuary of St. Patrick's Cathedral. As mentioned earlier, the Pope warmly embraced Sheen and told him that he had spoken and written well about Jesus and was a loyal son of the Church. On his sixtieth anniversary in the priesthood, Sheen received a letter from the Pope expressing his good wishes and congratulations, part of which said:

> God called you to proclaim in an extraordinary way his dynamic word. With great zeal you accepted this call, and directed your many talents to spreading the Gospel of Jesus Christ. Thus, in the six decades of your priestly service, God has touched the lives of millions

---

[3] *Ibid.*, pp. 292-293.
[4] *Ibid.*, pp. 236-237.

of men and women of our time. They have listened to you on radio, watched you on television, profited from your many literary achievements and participated in spiritual conferences conducted by you. And so with Saint Paul, "I thank God whenever I think of you; and every time I pray for you, I pray with joy, remembering how you have helped spread the Good News" (Ph 1:3-4).... I ask you to pray for me and for the success of my ministry as universal pastor of the Church.

Sheen responded to the Pope one month later:

After the greeting extended me by Your Holiness at Saint Patrick's Cathedral, and the beautiful letter on my Sixtieth Anniversary, were it not for the renewed strength the Lord gave me, I should have sung my "*Nunc Dimittis*." But I am still, thank God, blessed with the Psalmist's promise: "Vigorous in old age like a tree full of sap" (92:14). ... Pray for Your Holiness? That I always do for the Vicar of Christ, but in this fourth cycle of a crisis which strikes the Body of Christ every five hundred years, I pray for Your Holiness as for another Gregory the Great, Gregory VII, Pius V, and for our times as the poet Slowacki put it: "A Slav Pope who will sweep out the churches and make them clean within." Every night when silence gives vision scope, I pray to Our Lord in the Blessed Sacrament for the Chief Shepherd of our souls, and the only moral authority left in the world.... I wish I were younger to enjoy the blessings to come, for as one of our poets put it: "Lift up thy head and hark. What sounds there are in the dark, for his feet are coming to thee on the waters."

Sheen believed that there were four periods of crisis for the Church since the birth of Christ. The first cycle of crisis was

during the fall of Rome. A Benedictine monk who had been a
Roman senator became Pope and reigned under the name Gregory (later known as Gregory the Great). He undertook the conversion of the barbarians and prepared the way for a Christian
Europe. The second cycle of crisis began around 1000 A.D.
There was the Eastern Schism but also a decline of holiness in
the Church. Clerical concubinage, simony and the naming of
bishops by Princes and Kings were rampant in the Church.
Pope Gregory VII, another Benedictine, sought to correct the
abuses. The third crisis came with the Reformation. Some
sought to reform the Church from within and some just left and
began their own Churches. Sheen points out that there was
nothing wrong with the faith at that time; what really needed
reform was behavior. Pope Pius V, a Dominican, implemented
the reforms of the Council of Trent and established missionary
activity throughout the world. In 1979, Sheen stated that we are
now in the fourth cycle of five hundred years. This crisis is
rooted in a false mysticism:

> … we are in the fourth cycle of five hundred years, with
> two world wars in twenty-one years, and the univer-
> sal dread of nuclear incineration…. Our times have
> seen the rise of the Red mysticism of class and party
> in communism, the Black mysticism of the state under
> fascism, and the Brown mysticism of the race under
> Nazism. In other parts of the world, a false mystique
> uncoiled like a serpent suffocated freedom of speech
> and suppressed opposition and assassinated those who
> differed.

He asserted that John Paul would offer the world a *"mystique without a politique."* Sheen believed the mystique that John
Paul would offer in the coming years would be based on human freedom. Freedom to do — not whatever you want — but

freedom to do what you *ought* to do: "oughtness" that implied a goal, a purpose in living and a meaning. A mystique that would affirm the sacredness of human life, the right to worship God according to the light of conscience and a commitment to human rights. John Paul's message would appeal to those whose hands are full but whose hearts are empty. Those who suffer from hunger of the spirit while much of the world suffers from hunger of the body: "The spiritual in a man dressed in white would appeal to those who have found their way. He has become their guide in faith and morals; to all who have lost their way he becomes a beacon of hope." Though Sheen witnessed less than a year of John Paul's Pontificate, he believed that history would judge the Pope as one of the greatest to occupy the Chair of St. Peter.[5]

---

[5] *Ibid.*, passim, pp. 242-246.

10

Ecumenist

FOR MANY NON-CATHOLICS, SHEEN WAS THEIR ONLY CONTACT WITH the Catholic Church. Therefore, many would base their judgments about the Church primarily on Sheen.[1] Interestingly enough, Sheen received more letter from Jews, rather than from Protestants and Catholics. The immense popularity of his television program contributed to the feeling that Sheen had mastered this new medium of communication. Sheen appealed to the common man and was considered an alternative to Billy Graham and Norman Vincent Peale, who were, at the time, considered the voices of Protestantism.[2]

Even before his television show, Sheen was an influence on those not of the Catholic faith. And as stated earlier, Sheen's main attempt was not proselytizing, but the saving of souls, though he welcomed as a by-product any conversions to the Church due to anything he might have said or done.[3] As writer, Mark Massa points out, though Sheen's television show was

---

[1] *TIC*, p. 73. Also, see John Jay Daly, "The Man Behind the Mike," *The Sign*, May 10, 1945, p. 510.

[2] J.P. Dolan in his book, *The American Catholic Experience*, Doubleday and Co., Garden City, NY, 1985, p. 393. Dolan calls Sheen a "true Catholic hero" and asserts that Billy Graham believed that Sheen was "one of the greatest preachers of our century." Cited in a footnote by Kathleen Riley Fields, "Fulton J. Sheen: An American Catholic Response to the Twentieth Century," dissertation, Notre Dame University, South Bend, IN, 1989. p. 369.

[3] See p. 20 of this book.

perceived as ecumenical, "the not-so-hidden subtext of Sheen's message was relentlessly Catholic, Thomistic, and neo-scholastic."[4]

Basically, the television medium was a way for Sheen to get people to change not by telling them want they wanted to hear but what they needed to hear. Sheen was concerned about ecumenism long before it came into vogue. In 1944, Sheen published *Love One Another*.[5] This book addressed ecumenical concerns and issues twenty years prior to the attention they received at the Second Vatican Council. Sheen calls for cooperation among all men of good will for the sake of the country. Anticipating an end to the war, Sheen was now asking for the good will of all men for the sake of religious harmony. He held that intolerance was something that should be alien to all creeds. Tolerance, however, does not mean that we neglect or exclude truth.

> Indifference means the denial of the distinction between the true and the false, right and wrong. Confusing charity and tolerance, it gives an equal hearing, for example, to speech which advocates the freedom to murder and to speech which advocates the freedom to live. Indifference is never a stable condition, but passes into polarization.[6]

---

[4] Mark S. Massa, *Catholics and American Culture; Fulton Sheen, Dorothy Day, and the Notre Dame Football Team*, Crossroad Publishing Company, New York, 1999, p. 97.

[5] Sheen, *Love One Another*, Garden City Books, New York, 1953; originally published in 1944 by P.J. Kenedy & Sons. "Monsignor Sheen's latest book takes its place with those works seeking to provide an answer to current social problems. *Love One Another* provides the answer. The book easily excels. We find chapters on the friendship of Christians with Jews and Jews with Christians, of Catholics with Protestants and of non-Catholics with Catholics, and a chapter on friendship with all peoples, races and classes. This book has other reasons to commend it. It is timely." *Catholic Education Review*, Vol. 43:181.

[6] Sheen, *Missions and the World Crisis*, Bruce Publishing Co., Milwaukee, WI, p. 7.

The theme of *Love One Another* was friendship between Christians and Jews, Catholics and Protestants and all peoples, races, colors. Love of neighbor should be based on love of God.[7] Sheen emphasized that differences between Catholics and Protestants are lover's quarrels, similar to a husband and wife fighting over a damaged fender or a high meat bill. But their love for one another should not be in question. Neither should their mutual love for Christ.[8] Anti-Christianity and anti-Semitism on the part of any institution or individual are the criteria of mutual failure to be what they claim to be, namely, religious. Hatred of someone from another faith is deemed by Sheen an offense against the Creator and a result of the person not confronting the "internal causes" of his/her own misery — sins and forgetfulness of the moral law of God.

In his post-war writings, Sheen addressed the problems of everyday life for individuals as well as the challenges that the world was facing. The following books were intended by Sheen to respond to the needs and concern of the day: *Preface to Religion*[9]; *Lift Up Your Heart*[10]; *The Way to Happiness*[11]; *The Way*

---

[7] Sheen's commitment to ecumenism while serving as Bishop of Rochester will be addressed in Chapters 13 and 18.

[8] David Kucharsky, "Bottom-Line Theology: An Interview with Fulton J. Sheen," *Christianity Today* 21, June 3, 1977, pp. 8-11.

[9] Sheen, *Preface to Religion*, P.J. Kenedy & Sons, Inc., New York, 1946.

[10] *Lift Up Your Heart*, McGraw-Hill Book Co., New York, 1950. Sheen discusses and analyzes the inner life of modern man. "This book is Bishop Sheen at his best. It can be read with great profit by very many in this hectic age." *Jackson Sun.* "The book sparkles with modern comparisons and the shrewd use of analogy... [it] will be read and treasured by thousands." *Pittsburgh Press. Lift Up Your Heart* was re-published by Liguori Publications in 1997.

[11] *The Way to Happiness*, Garden City Books, Garden City, NY, 1954. It was re-published by Alba House in 1997.

to *Inner Peace*[12]; *Life of Christ*[13]; *Go to Heaven*[14]; and a five volume set: *Life is Worth Living.*[15] *Peace of Soul, Life of Christ, The Eternal Galilean*[16], and *Life is Worth Living* were all best sellers. In his

---

[12] *Way to Inner Peace*, Garden City Books, Garden City, NY, 1955. Re-published by Alba House in 1995, Staten Island, New York. The book is described thus by the editor: "In this work, written some fifty years ago, we find many nearly forgotten age-old truths surprisingly and specifically apropos to the needs of our own times. Rich in psychology and richer yet in New Testament spirituality, these pages will provide an invaluable guide to all those who, for whatever reason, are seeking the way to inner peace."

[13] *Life of Christ*, McGraw-Hill Book Co., New York, 1958. In a review of *Life of Christ*, Harold C. Gardiner wrote, "No one will fail to hear in this synthesis an eloquent voice which is saying again for our times, and in contemporary rhetoric, what the great Fathers of the early Church said for their flocks. Bishop Sheen has one advantage over a St. Augustine — the 'flock' that will read this book will undoubtedly be many times larger than that which heard or read the Bishop of Hippo." See "The Meaning for Our Day," *New York Times*, October 19, 1958. Also, "Of the many titles which have poured from Sheen's pen this may well become the most popular and most influential. In view of the subject matter and its inspiring treatment, it deserves that distinction." *America.* "Although the author is a Roman Catholic, the long work will be of interest to Christians of all denominations." *Booklist. Life of Christ* was re-published in 1977 with an updated preface.

[14] *Go to Heaven*, McGraw-Hill Book Co., Inc., New York, London & Toronto, 1960.

[15] This series of books is taken from scripts of Sheen's television series: *Life is Worth Living.* In his preface for the first volume, Sheen wrote: "In this spirit we offer these telecasts to the public, in the fervent hope that they may draw at least one soul closer to God; if they do that, the author will feel he is fulfilling in a small way the vocation to which the Good Lord has called him. Let it never be said again that it is difficult to write a book. It is now proven that if a person talks only an hour a week for twenty-six weeks, he already has enough material for a book. This is how this book was written" (p. ix, vii). McGraw-Hill Book Co., New York. First Series, 1953. Second Series, 1954. Third Series, 1955. Fourth Series, 1956. Fifth Series, 1957.

[16] *The Eternal Galilean*, Appleton-Century Co., Inc., New York and London, 1934; in the introduction, we read the following: "This book is intended to serve a double purpose: first, it seeks to be an antidote to those vague, sentimental lives of Christ, which picture Him merely as a Teacher of humanitarian ethics, a world reformer, a sentimental moralist, or a founder of a new world religion, and hence to be ranked equally with Buddha, Confucius and Socrates; secondly, it seeks to show how Christ is unique in the history of the world."In a review found in *Catholic Historical Review* we read: "In this book Bishop Sheen tells the story of the Son of God. But he does more than relate history; he portrays some of the characteristics of the Eternal Galilean — that Divine Person made Man in Nazareth. An occasional play on words, a well-tuned sentence, an excellent choice of words throughout, combine to make this learned work a pleasant, and almost poetic, piece of soteriological literature." *The Eternal Galilean* was re-published by Alba House, Staten Island, New York, in 1997.

Life of Christ, Sheen returned to emphasizing the importance of the cross in our daily lives and in the life of Christ:

> It is hoped that sweet intimacy with the Crucified Christ, during what I know now were the most blessed days of my life, will break through these pages and give to the reader the lesson I learned... that every tribulation is, "The Shade of His Hand outstretched caressingly."[17]

In *Peace of Soul*, published in 1949, Sheen stated his belief that man is divided from himself, his fellow man and from God.[18] This alienation causes the problems the world is facing, including the fear of worldwide destruction from the atomic bomb. Mankind was looking for answers in the wrong places, in the secular realm rather than in the spiritual. Man denies personal guilt and relies upon himself rather than God.

> The tormented minds of today are not the effects of our tormented world; it is our upset minds that have upset the world. There is no such thing as the problem of the atomic bomb; there is, rather, the problem of the man who makes and uses it. Only men and nations whose personalities were already atomized could join forces with external nature to use an atomic bomb in

---

[17] Sheen, *Life of Christ*, Image Books: Garden City, NY, 1977, p. 11.

[18] *Peace of Soul*, Image Books, Garden City, NY, 1949, p. 7. *Peace of Soul* was re-published by Liguori Publications in 1996. Robert E. Brennan, in a review of *Peace of Soul*, wrote the following: "For more than a quarter of a century, the stream of solid Catholic apologetic has been flowing from the pen of Fulton Sheen. The source of his inspiration has been mainly two: Holy Writ and the teaching of St. Thomas Aquinas. In his books and sermons, Sheen has stood as a bulwark against paganism of every sort, as a friend of those in search of the truth, a guide for the bewildered who are looking for a way of life that will lead to happiness and ultimate salvation." See *New Scholasticism*, Vol. 24, January, 1950, p. 86.

an attack on human existence. Man, by attempting to exist either apart from God or defiant of God, has made the world as delirious as his own mind is neurotic. It is man who has to be remade *first*; then society will be remade by the restored new man.[19]

[19] *Ibid.*, p. 244.

11

The Missions

THE MONSIGNOR IS WELL QUALIFIED FOR THE IMPORTANT work of heading the Propagation of the Faith in this country. His many and outstanding talents of heart and mind will henceforth be directed to an all-embracing apostolate. Missionaries in the far-flung outposts of the Catholic Church will find in him a zeal that matches their own. In a sense, the Monsignor's parish is the world and his parishioners the people of the earth. Many souls have been enlightened and strengthened by Monsignor Sheen's zealous apostolate within the limits of the United States. His ardor will now have wider horizons to pursue in missionary work at a time when the Church will depend more and more upon Catholics in the United States for the support of her missions in foreign lands.[1]

In 1950, Fulton Sheen was appointed National Director of the Society for the Propagation of the Faith by Pope Pius XII.[2] For thirty-one years, Sheen had served as priest, teacher, preacher and evangelist. Sheen was already well acquainted with spreading the faith. Now, he would represent the Church

---

[1] *Ave Maria*, Vol. 72, October 7, 1950, p. 452.
[2] *TIC*, p. 232.

not only in the United States but throughout the world. On a visit to Sydney, Australia, Sheen recalls arriving with Francis Cardinal Spellman. Spellman made the following remarks:

> A word about Monsignor Sheen, who in America is doing more than any Archbishop or any bishop to make the faith known and loved. He is one of the most truly apostolic souls of our times. He has the ear of Catholics; he has the ear of non-Catholics, and I rejoice to know that the Australians love him as much as we do."[3]

As director, Sheen was given an opportunity to minister to troubled souls everywhere. Because of his new responsibilities, Sheen resigned his professorship at Catholic University. About a year later, on June 11, 1951, Sheen was ordained an Auxiliary Bishop of the Archdiocese of New York, "through the good graces of Cardinal Spellman."[4] The "missionary with the mike" would now be heard on distant shores where the Church was attempting both to alleviate the poverty of the faithful and to evangelize local populations. His popularity served him well in trying to enhance the image of the Propagation and in raising monies in order that the Society could accomplish its work, including numerous charities.

Of note was Sheen's own personal concern for the poor. As a young priest, Sheen did parish work in a poor neighborhood at St. Patrick's Parish, in Soho, London, England. The parish was half Italian and half Irish with some Chinese. Monies Sheen received from speaking engagements and royalties from books were quickly dispersed among different charities.

---

[3] *Ibid.*, pp. 135-136.
[4] *Ibid.*, p. 92.

For example, the Blessed Martin De Porres Hospital in Mobile, Alabama, a 315-bed institution for Blacks, was built with monies donated by Sheen from his personal funds.[5] His good work was done with the realization that Christ had already acted before him: "Every great deed done to a neighbor is done in a world in which Christ has already acted: touching lepers, filling food baskets, healing withered hands. Only when we align ourselves with Him do all our good deeds begin to work."[6]

While serving as National Director of the Society for the Propagation of the Faith, Sheen raised over $100 million, two-thirds of which came from the United States alone. In 1966, during his last year as National Director for the Society, $16,000,000 was raised.[7] These funds were used to support 300,000 missionaries, 150,000 schools, 26,000 hospitals, 5,000 orphanages and 400 leper colonies.[8] During those sixteen years, letters of support, financial and otherwise poured into his office every day, averaging between eighteen and twenty-five thousand.[9]

Sheen believed that it was the purpose of missionaries not so much to bring Christ to others as to bring Christ *out* of them, "The good Hindu, the good Buddhist, the good Confucianist, the good Muslim are all saved by Christ, not by Buddhism, etc., but through their sacraments, their prayers, their asceticism, their morality, their good life."[10] During his travels, Sheen became even more aware of the plight of many peoples. The level

---

[5] James C.G. Conniff, *The Bishop Sheen Story*, Fawcett Publications, Greenwich, CT, 1953, p. 29.

[6] *Those Mysterious Priests*, p. 244.

[7] John Tracy Ellis, *American Catholicism*, University of Chicago Press, Chicago, IL, 1969, p. 252.

[8] *New York Times*, November 6, 1966.

[9] *TIC*, p. 110.

[10] *Ibid.*, p. 148.

of poverty both spiritually and materially that he witnessed was overwhelming.

> One cannot spend fifteen or more years serving in un-
> derdeveloped nations and the poor of the world by
> begging for them without developing an entirely new
> point of view with regard to the world. I begin to think
> less of the problem of poverty and more of the poor;
> less of the problem of crime and more of the criminal;
> less about age and more about service to a stranger
> who lives with the slum dwellers who have no place
> to lay their heads. Travel merely confirms the teaching
> of theology that humanity is one. The accidental dif-
> ferences of color and race and what jingles in the pocket
> are of little concern. The longer I live the more I become
> convinced that in the face of injustices we must begin
> to say I love. Kind deeds are not enough. We must learn
> to say I forgive.[11]

What Sheen saw and experienced would cause him to change his outlook. He claimed that the change was reflected in all aspects of his work during those years, including his books and columns and the subject matter for his television shows. Sheen's travels confirmed the teachings of the Church that humanity is one. His trips to the Third World, however, shifted his stress from ideology to economics, politics and the social order.[12] In musing about his years as Director at the Propagation of the Faith, Sheen had this to say:

> What the appointment as National Director brought to
> my life was the opportunity to see that Christian sal-

---

[11] *Ibid.*, pp. 151-152.
[12] *Ibid.*, p. 149.

This 1930's photo of the Sheen family shows the close knit family: Mr. and Mrs. Newton Sheen and their four sons (l. to r.) Joseph, Fulton, Aloysius and Thomas. (Courtesy, Fulton J. Sheen Archives)

Sheen had just turned 18 when he graduated from Spalding Institute in Peoria, Illinois. The year was 1913. (Courtesy, Fulton J. Sheen Archives)

Sheen was ordained in 1919 at the age of 24. (Courtesy, Fulton J. Sheen Archives)

"The Catholic Hour" featuring Fulton J. Sheen was broadcast on NBC radio during the 1930's. (Courtesy, Fulton J. Sheen Archives)

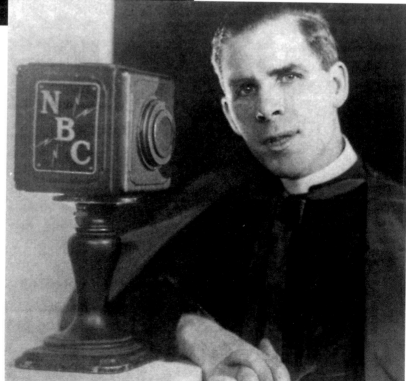

CATHOLIC EVIDENCE GUILD

QUESTIONS
CHEERFULLY
ANSWERED

Sheen was a guest street preacher of the Catholic Evidence Guild
in Alabama in the 1930's. (Courtesy, Fulton J. Sheen Archives)

Milton Berle, Sheen and Mayor Vincent R. Impellitteri of New York during a telethon in 1950. (Courtesy, Society for the Propagation of the Faith)

Sheen and Ed Sullivan on the occasion of the Look Award, Sunday, December 30, 1956. (Courtesy, Society for the Propagation of the Faith)

May, 1951, Munich, Germany. Msgr. Sheen talks for Armed Forces. (Air Force photo)

Sheen never visited Europe without paying a visit to Lourdes. (Courtesy, Society for the Propagation of the Faith)

Solemn moments in Rome's church of Sts. John and Paul in June, 1951, when Adeodato Giovanni Cardinal Piazza consecrated Sheen as Auxiliary Bishop of New York. (G. Felici)

Sheen was famous for his use of the blackboard on his "Life Is Worth Living" television series. (New York News photo)

On November 11, 1956, Sheen celebrated a Byzantine Liturgy at Holy Cross Cathedral in Boston. (Courtesy, Society for the Propagation of the Faith)

Fulton J. Sheen, Pope Pius XII, and Msgr. Edward T. O'Meara in June, 1957. (Courtesy, Society for the Propagation of the Faith)

Sheen commissioned several Maryknoll Sisters for overseas missionary service in May, 1957. (Courtesy, Society for the Propagation of the Faith)

On November 27, 1960 Sheen was visiting the missions in Sasolburg, South Africa. (Courtesy, Society for the Propagation of the Faith)

With Pope John XXIII in the Pope's study. (G. Felici)

Sheen took part in the Second Vatican Council, "one of the great blessings the Lord has bestowed on my life." (Courtesy, Society for the Propagation of the Faith)

Sheen spoke to a half-million men at a midnight Mass commemorating the 400th anniversary of the arrival of Christianity in the Philippines, 1965. (Courtesy, Society for the Propagation of the Faith)

The new Bishop of Rochester (1966) gives his first press interview.
(Courtesy, Society for the Propagation of the Faith)

In 1969 Sheen offered his resignation to Pope Paul VI during this audience.
(Courtesy, Society for the Propagation of the Faith)

Archbishop Sheen accepts Catholic Actors Guild Award in his first public appearance after open-heart surgery, November 1977, at the Hilton Hotel. (Chris Sheridan. The Catholic News)

John Paul II embraces Archbishop Sheen at St. Patrick's
Cathedral, October 2, 1979, two months before his death.
(Associated Press photo)

Sheen often found himself in the spotlight, and he knew how
to handle it well. (Courtesy, Society for the Propagation of
the Faith)

vation has both an earthly and an historical dimension;
that the conversion of a single soul may not be alienated from the promotion of human rights as required
by the Gospel, and which is central to our ministry; that
soul-winning and society-saving are the concave and
convex side of the love of God and love of neighbor;
that in addition to begetting children of God through
evangelization, we have to give the witness of frater-
nal love in a sensitiveness toward humanity's desire
for freedom and justice; that as Christ was both divine
and human, so the mission of every Christian is to be
transcendent in lifting eyes to Heaven but also immi-
nent in the way that he lives on earth; that earthly liberation is an integral part of evangelization and that
they are as united as Creation and Redemption.[13]

Sheen was succeeded by Bishop Edward T. O'Meara, who
later gave the eulogy at Sheen's funeral. The two men first met
by chance at St. Louis Cathedral. After a meeting of the directors of the Society, they decided to make a visit to the Blessed
Sacrament. The Cathedral was closed. Sheen ran into then
Monsignor O'Meara, who opened and turned on the lights in
the Cathedral for the directors. Sheen thought his gesture was
very kind and gracious. Sheen wrote O'Meara's bishop and
asked if he would permit the Monsignor to become Assistant
National Director of the Society. Thus, as Sheen describes it,
"Providence prepared the way for the well-being of the Propagation of the Faith by a seeming chance meeting with a priest
before the closed door of the St. Louis Cathedral."[14]

William J. McCormack, present National Director of the

---

[13] *Ibid.,* p. 108.
[14] *Ibid.,* p. 109.

Propagation of the Faith, expressed to me a profound respect and admiration for all that Bishop Sheen accomplished in, as the bishop described it, his "broad apostolate." Bishop McCormack trumpeted Sheen as a "prophet of those days," who was, "in a biblical way, open to being an instrument of the Lord. He was sent by the Lord with a message to give, whether anyone wanted to listen to it or not." Bishop McCormack also saw Sheen as a prophet in a secondary sense, in that he predicted "the tremendous growth and expansion of the Church in Africa. He also tried to warn us that a contraceptive mentality would lead to abortion, abortion to euthanasia, and both would lead to unprecedented violence throughout society." Bishop McCormack maintains that Sheen was warning us of the consequences of this mentality long before these problems became the issues that they are today: "That violence which he predicted as a consequence of contraception, abortion and euthanasia is now prevalent throughout our society and is a fact of life."[15]

Contraception, so widely practiced in the West, which many believe to be *the* cure for what ails many of the poorer countries was deemed by Sheen in 1933, "a betrayal of life and love's great trust." He went on to claim that couples who use birth control are unfaithful to the gift of love and are like "artists who are always picking up brushes but never finishing a picture; always lifting chisels but never producing a statue; always touching bow to string, but never emitting a harmony."[16] The "violence" that Sheen predicted is taking place in a nuclear age when man could easily destroy every living thing including himself. Plagues, famine and disease afflict man and the vio-

---

[15] Interview with Bishop William J. McCormack by author on November 15, 1997.
[16] Sheen, *The Hymn of the Conquered* (New York: Garden City Books, 1933), p. 68.

lence, that once was witnessed and reserved for the battlefield, has now reached into our classrooms. Some ask where God is in all this? A better question might be, "What else should we expect since God has been removed from the classroom?" Protests of horror at random acts of violence are not enough. What must happen is the affirmation of the worth of a person as a creature of God.

Sheen submits that God *is* present in the midst of man's suffering. The problem is that Christians, some with good intentions, some not, have isolated Christ from His Cross. Thus, man hears either of a Christless Cross or a Crossless Christ. According to Sheen, neither is true, because Christ cannot be separated from His Cross and the cross from Christ anymore than He can be separated from His Resurrection. Sheen insists that if God allowed His own Son to suffer, why should others be exempt? Familiarity with the missions equipped him well for his participation in what was totally unexpected — Pope John XXIII's call for an Ecumenical Council.

12

The Second Vatican Council

S HEEN WAS JUST AS SURPRISED AS EVERYONE ELSE WHEN POPE JOHN XXIII called for an Ecumenical Council. While visiting with the Pope, John XXIII related to Sheen how he had decided to call the Council. It was just outside his private chapel that John received his "inspiration." He told Sheen, "I knew very well that the Cardinals would say, 'Oh you are too old to hold a Council,' or 'There are too many conflicts in the Church,' so I called in my secretary, Monsignor Capovilla, and said: 'We will go out to the Church of St. Paul Outside the Walls and announce the Vatican Council and then no one can stop it.'"[1]

On Christmas Day, 1961, the Pope issued *Humanae Salutis* calling for a Second Vatican Council. Sheen was named to two Commissions: the Conciliar Commission on the Missions and the pre-conciliar Catholic Action Committee.[2] His contribution consisted of applying his expertise on the Missions during discourses and in the interventions he submitted on several subjects. Those subjects included ecumenism, religious freedom, education, priestly formation, and the Decree on the Church's Missionary Activity.[3] Sheen petitioned the Commission that the

---

[1] *TIC*, p. 236.

[2] *Ibid.*

[3] Kathleen Riley Fields, "Fulton J. Sheen: An American Catholic Response to the Twentieth Century," doctoral dissertation, Notre Dame University, South Bend, IN, 1989, p. 421.

Congregation for the Propagation of the Faith change its name. Sheen was concerned that the word for propaganda in Latin, had a bad connotation. Sheen recounts that his suggestion was rejected because it was felt that it showed little respect for a congregation that had existed for three centuries. It should be noted that not long after the Council ended, the name of the congregation *was* changed to the Congregation for the Evangelization of Peoples. As a result of Sheen's worldwide travels, as head of the Propagation, many of the cardinals and bishops attending the Council, found "the one bishop they all knew, the missionary's friend, the lover of the poor."[4]

In his travels throughout the world, Sheen saw the necessity of the Church's being involved in the lives of peoples and nations. Pope John XXIII expressed the same conviction and the reasons for this involvement in *Humanae Salutis*, "in order to contribute more efficaciously to the solution of the problems of the modern age." At the Council, several members of the Catholic Action Committee wanted to include a chapter on Tourism. Sheen could see no value in it unless it was to remind the faithful about attendance at the Holy Eucharist on Sundays and Holy Days of Obligation. Sheen believed that he was the only Conciliar Father who, before the Council, asked that there could be a chapter on women: "I had a strong conviction that the feminine principle in religion had been neglected. Many world religions were without the feminine principle and we were beginning to live in an age when women were coming into their own. I still feel that it would have been well to have included a chapter on women; it certainly was far more impor-

---

4   P. David Finks, "Crisis in Smugtown: A Study of Conflict, Churches and Citizen Organizations in Rochester, New York, 1964-1969," doctoral dissertation, Union Graduate School of the Union for Experimenting Colleges and Universities, Rochester, NY, 1975, p. 182.

tant than tourism."[5] Since the Council, numerous Church documents on women and their role in the Church and society have been published.

In commenting about the Council, Sheen notes that it was necessary for the Council to strike a balance between the world and the Church: *individualism* and *socialism*.[6] He believed that the Council tried to establish an equilibrium between evangelization and human progress, between soul winning and society-saving, between divine salvation and human liberation. Sheen notes that "for the first time in the history of all the Councils of the Church there was a chapter on 'The World,' in which the Council wanted to stress *the unity of creation and redemption*; and the truth that the dignity and freedom of the human person is inseparable from salvation."[7] He believed that it was this attempt to strike a balance between the *spiritual and social* and the Church's *being in* and yet *not of* the world, that led to tensions between "the conservatives and the worldlings."[8]

Tensions that occurred after the Council were not a surprise to Sheen because one had only to look at the whole history of the Church to find that, during a Council, there is the "outpouring of the Holy Spirit" followed by "an extra show of force by the anti-spirit or the demonic." Indeed, Sheen believed that, had *not* the "turbulence" occurred, "one might almost doubt the operation of the Third Person of the Trinity over the Assembly." On a personal note, Sheen declares that, "To have been present at the Council and have had a part in it was one of the great blessings the Lord bestowed upon me in my life."[9]

---

[5] *TIC*, p. 284.
[6] *Ibid.*, p. 289.
[7] *Ibid.*, p. 290.
[8] *Ibid.*
[9] *Ibid.*, p. 281.

13

The Episcopacy

A S A YOUNG PRIEST, SHEEN PRAYED THAT ONE DAY HE MIGHT BECOME a bishop, quoting the words of St. Paul who wrote: "It is an honorable ambition to aspire to be a bishop." He hoped that his desire would come about through the intercession of Mary:

> What was clearly the motive was the desire to be a successor to the Apostles. I do not remember exactly when, but I do believe it was during my first or second year of graduate work at the University of Louvain. I remember the form the petition took. On the way to class, I passed the Church of St. Michael. On the walls there were paintings of the Seven Dolors of the Blessed Mother. A Hail Mary at each of the Seven Dolors was offered for that intention, and I have continued that prayer though I have been a bishop for many years. Along with that prayer to God went a resolution never to do anything by myself, or to cultivate any friendship, or to use any means to achieve that "honorable ambition."[1]

After one year as Director of the Society for the Propagation of the Faith, Fulton J. Sheen was ordained Auxiliary Bishop of New York in the Church of Saint John and Paul in Rome on

---

[1] Sheen, *TIC*, p. 91.

June 11, 1951. Fifteen years later, in 1966 at the age of seventy-one, Sheen was appointed Bishop of Rochester, New York, by Pope Paul VI. No one is sure just why Sheen was appointed to Rochester but there was speculation that Cardinal Spellman was behind the appointment because he wanted Sheen out of New York.

As to why Spellman would want Sheen out of New York, we have to go back to 1957. A rift began between Spellman and Sheen during Sheen's tenure as director of the Society for the Propagation of the Faith. Author John Cooney asserted that "Spellman would dip into Propagation funds to help his own pet charities and those of his friends. This irritated Sheen, who thought that money sent to the Propagation should be spent solely by the Propagation."[2] In 1957, Spellman delegated to the Propagation the distribution of millions of dollars of surplus milk obtained from the U.S. government. Spellman wanted the Propagation to pay for the milk. Sheen refused. Apparently, there was no agreement to disagree. Sheen appealed to Rome, claiming that Spellman had received the milk for free. Both men were called to Rome to settle the matter. They both presented their case before Pope Pius XII. Washington was consulted and said that, indeed, the milk was given to the Archdiocese gratis. The Pope resolved the matter in Sheen's favor. Spellman was upset at the decision and believed that Sheen caused him to lose face with his mentor and friend, the Pope. The relationship between Sheen and Spellman never really recovered from this incident.[3]

---

[2]   John Cooney, *The American Pope*, Times Books, New York, 1984, p. 254.

[3]   A relationship that had once been close and caused Sheen to autograph the following in his book, *Three to Get Married*, which he presented to the Cardinal on May 15, 1951: "To His Eminence Francis Cardinal Spellman. In token of thanksgiving greater than words can tell, and in promise of loyalty and devotion which deeds, with God's grace, will prove." In 1988, I purchased the book from the library at St. Joseph's Seminary, Dunwoodie, New York.

Father Robert I. Gannon, S.J., who gave the eulogy at Spellman's funeral and was his biographer, described Spellman as, "a complex and positive character, the wrong man to cross when he decided he was right and you were wrong." It is important to note, however, that Gannon also described Spellman as first and foremost, a faithful and devoted priest.[4]

Father Noonan made these observations concerning the "feud," as he called it, between Spellman and Sheen: "Pius (XII) was very close to Spellman. Spellman must have certainly prevailed on Pius not to promote his stubborn, but extremely gifted underling; he never succeeded Spellman as Archbishop of New York. (Pope) John (XXIII) was a very astute man, full of charity. He gave many priests audiences. To Sheen at one such audience he remarked that he knew all about the Sheen-Spellman donnybrook." Paradoxically, Noonan quotes Spellman, at a luncheon honoring Sheen on the day of his installation as bishop, as saying that he had mixed feelings of sorrow and joy at Bishop Sheen's new appointment. At the luncheon, Spellman told Sheen: "You belong not only to the ages but to the world."[5]

Because of what had happened between Spellman and Sheen, it is not surprising that many believed Spellman was behind Sheen's appointment to Rochester. Sheen never spoke publicly about his appointment to Rochester, in contrast to his giving Spellman the credit for his appointment as an Auxiliary Bishop of New York. Nor did he speak publicly about his disagreements with Spellman.[6]

---

[4] Reverend Florence D. Cohalan, *A Popular History of the Archdiocese of New York,* United States Catholic Historical Society, Yonkers, NY, 1983, p. 326.

[5] See D.P. Noonan, *The Passion of Fulton Sheen,* Our Sunday Visitor, Huntington, IN, 1975. See pp. 119-120, 122, 72, 74, 139, in that order.

[6] As to why Sheen never commented publicly about his problems with Cardinal Spellman and other clerics, see Chapter 17 and p. 121 of this book.

Bishop Patrick V. Ahern, Secretary to Cardinal Spellman from 1957-1966 and now retired Auxiliary Bishop of New York, contrary to the common opinion of the time, believed Spellman was not behind Sheen's appointment to Rochester. He bases his belief on a conversation he had with Spellman early on the night before the announcement of Sheen's appointment. Bishop Ahern related the following: "He (Spellman) told me that Sheen was going to be the new bishop of Rochester and asked me what I thought of the appointment, to which I replied that I thought it was a poor one. Spellman asked me why, to which I responded, 'It would be a waste of his talents. He is a great evangelist for the Church. As ordinary of a diocese, he would be hindered from that work because of his responsibilities.'" Spellman agreed with Ahern's assessment and told Bishop Ahern (then a Monsignor) he did everything he could to stop the appointment. Ahern asked Spellman if he had tried to stop it, why wasn't it stopped, to which Spellman replied, "Because he's (Sheen) *numero uno* with *numero uno*," namely Pope Paul VI. Concerning the notion that Spellman was behind the appointment because of the friction between the two, Bishop Ahern stated that he is certain that Spellman was not behind Sheen's appointment adding, "In addition to what he told me, I simply don't remember his ever acting vindictively. Cardinal Spellman and Bishop Sheen were originally very good friends. Spellman even bought Fulton (upon being named a Monsignor) his new Monsignor robes!" Bishop Ahern added that he could not recall Spellman ever having said anything negative about Sheen.[7] This was confirmed by Bishop Broderick who added

---

[7] Bishop Patrick V. Ahern, Auxiliary Bishop of New York, author of *Maurice and Thérèse: A Love Story*, 1998, interviewed by author, New York City, July 2, 1999. Comments made by Sheen to Father Andrew Apostoli, concerning his appointment to Rochester seem to confirm Bishop Ahern's assessment. See p. 93 of this book.

that he didn't recall ever hearing Sheen comment negatively about Spellman.[8] These assertions by two priests who knew both men, Bishop Ahern, who was close to Spellman and Bishop Broderick, who was close to both, conflict with the speculation that the two men couldn't tolerate each other.

Others thought the assignment of Sheen to Rochester was an affront to a man of his stature, one whose prospects, prior to the controversy between Spellman and Sheen, made him popularly regarded in Church circles as successor to Spellman as Archbishop of New York.[9] As writer Kathleen Riley Fields points out, Sheen's appointment was thought by many to be a misuse of his talents.[10] No matter, both Sheen and the Rochester diocese were delighted. Each would have something to offer the other. Sheen relished the thought of being closer to the people and with priests in particular. Rochester would have as its bishop someone with a worldwide reputation who had the ear of the Pope. But the appointment to Rochester would be Sheen's first experience as a pastor. He realized that he would have much to do and learn.

The appointment to Rochester, within one year of the end of the Second Vatican Council, meant that Sheen would be one of the first post-conciliar bishops. He felt that he was being given a wonderful opportunity to implement the Council's reforms and set precedents for others to follow. Sheen claimed that he was "happy about the appointment and the job that awaited him."[11] He said, "What I'd wish to do would be the task

---

[8] Bishop Broderick interview.

[9] *Ibid.*, p. 74.

[10] Kathleen Riley Fields, "Fulton J. Sheen: An American Catholic Response to the Twentieth Century," doctoral dissertation, Notre Dame University, South Bend, IN, 1989, p. 443.

[11] *Ibid.*

of the implementation and putting into action the decrees of the Ecumenical Council."[12]

Rochester, in turn, was now the focus of worldwide attention because of its new bishop. Sheen would now be able to use his formidable talents in this little known diocese. Wherever he went, he made headlines, no longer in New York City or on distant shores but in upstate New York. Rather than live in the episcopal center, he moved into a special apartment at the Columbus Civic Center. He received the good wishes of the Right Reverend George M. Barrett, Episcopal Bishop, who described Sheen as a man who "understands modern life," and Rabbi Herbert Bronstein who described Sheen as "one of the gifted few who have been able meaningfully to interpret spiritual truths to the multitudes."[13]

In his first Pastoral Letter, Bishop Sheen stated his intention to implement the decrees of the Council, with emphasis on the spirit of poverty and ecumenism.[14] Always thought of as "conservative," he surprised many with his outreach to people of other faiths. *Time* described him as having the reputation of a Church conservative who was now a "highly imaginative innovator" appearing in Jewish synagogues and exhibiting concern for the poor.[15] Richard Hughes, executive director of the Rochester Council of Churches appreciated what the new bishop had done for F.I.G.H.T. (Freedom, Integration, God, Honor, Today) and described Sheen as "a man infused with the whole spirit of Catholic ecumenism."[16]

---

[12] Sheen, in an interview with Bob Considine, "Bishop Sheen's Great Joy — The Privilege to Serve," *World Journal Tribune* (New York), November 8, 1966.

[13] *Democrat and Chronicle*, December 11, 1966, cited by Kathleen Riley Fields, *op. cit.*, pp. 447-448.

[14] Sheen, "Pastoral Letter," April 28, 1967; in the Pastoral Letters File, Archives of the Diocese of Rochester.

[15] *Time*, February 10, 1967.

[16] *The Wall Street Journal*, September 12, 1967.

Given Sheen's position and various offices he held in the Church, it should come as no surprise that he would encounter clergymen of other faiths. Sheen recalled a humorous encounter with an Episcopalian clergyman while on a train trip from New York to Boston: "We began a friendly discussion on the validity of Anglican Orders. He contended he was a priest as much as I was, that he could offer the Holy Sacrifice of the Mass and that he could forgive sins. He was well versed in history and theology and our discussion proved to be so interesting that many passengers gathered around us to listen to the friendly debate. He got off the train at Providence. He advanced several steps, then turned around and, facing the audience which we both enjoyed, thought he would give me the last telling challenge by saying: 'Remember Sheen, I can do anything you can do.' I just had time to answer: 'No you can't. I can kiss your wife, but you can't kiss mine.'"[17] Another encounter he had on a train was with another Protestant clergyman, the Reverend Billy Graham. Graham remembers that Sheen was one of the first Catholic Bishops that he ever said a prayer with. Billy Graham referred to his encounter with Sheen as an "outstanding memory." Graham would often watch Sheen to learn from him how to communicate with a television audience. The way Billy Graham remembers the encounter is as follows:

> It was late at night when I heard a knock at the door of my compartment. I was so tired; I was already stretched out and decided not to answer because I had several people already who wanted to speak to me. But the knock persisted. I opened the door, and there stood Fulton Sheen. I was amazed and honored. He came in, we talked for nearly two hours. We talked about his

---

[17] *TIC*, p. 300.

ministry and mine and how different they were and yet how parallel they were. Our paths crossed on several occasions at dinners or receptions or conferences where we were both speakers. I have the fondest recollections of him. He was a man of God and a man of prayer.[18]

---

[18] Billy Graham, *Just As I Am*, Harper Collins Publishers, New York, NY, 1997, pp. 692-693. Also: George J. Marlin, *The Quotable Fulton Sheen*, Doubleday, New York, 1989, pp. 355-356.

14

Controversies

S HEEN WASTED NO TIME IN BECOMING INVOLVED IN CONTROVERSY within the diocese of Rochester. He became embroiled in a dispute between F.I.G.H.T. and the Eastman Kodak company over minority hiring practices. He created the position of Episcopal Vicar of Urban Ministry to deal with poverty and the urban plight of the poor.[1] Sheen believed that poverty was a "little pimple on our city's face," that needed to be removed. He made the following statement:

> The solution to this problem is not to be found in ignoring personal dignity. Nor is the solution to be found in trying to rally congregations into old boundaries, for stained glass windows are apt to becloud our vision of poverty and distress. Neither is the Church to be an Ivory Tower outside the Inner City. The Church must be where the problems are, where hunger is, where rooms are cold and where difficult decisions have to be made. The mission of the Church is to participate in Christ's suffering in the world, and to have even a

---

[1] "Sheen appointed Father P. David Finks to head the new office. Sheen decided to create the new office after "meeting with his clergy from the inner-city parishes. Sheen had become convinced that an imaginative, precedent-setting stroke was needed to draw attention to the plight of the urban poor." See Fields: "Fulton J. Sheen: An American Catholic Response to the Twentieth Century," doctoral dissertation, Notre Dame University, South Bend, IN, 1989, pp. 449-450.

kind of lovers' quarrel with those members who would
not feel the pain of the stripes on the backs of others.[2]

Sheen also appealed to industry and commerce leaders to
join with him in attempting to solve the problems of the poor.
Following riots during the Summer of 1964, Sheen appealed for
calm and warned that when the world looked at Rochester, it
was seeing not industry and commerce but its inner-city poverty.

Sheen realized shortly after arriving in Rochester, that he
needed episcopal assistance. As a way of emphasizing collegi-
ality with his priests, he invited them to send names to him of
priests who they thought should be auxiliary bishops, with the
assumption that "if the voice of the people can sometimes be
the voice of God, then certainly there are times when the voice
of the priesthood can be the voice of Christ."[3] The criteria he
emphasized to assist priests in making their recommendations
were: men who were known to be "spiritual, of sound moral
character, interested in the problems of the diocese and worthy of being called to the episcopacy." The result of this consultation and Sheen's recommendation to Pope Paul VI, was
the appointment of Bishop Denis Hickey and Bishop John
McCafferty, both described by Sheen as having "remarkable
good sense and were of inestimable help."[4]

Another precedent setting action by Sheen was the intro-

---

[2] Fulton Sheen, letter to Reverend Finks. This letter is preserved with Sheen's pa-
pers in the Archives and is categorized as "Document #3-D. January 3, 1967."
Caution is urged in reading something into the late bishop's statement concerning the Church and the world. While it is true Sheen wants the Church to be involved in the affairs of the world, namely, seeking the general welfare of all
peoples, this should not be done at the expense of the Church's primary mission,
namely, the saving of souls. See, *Those Mysterious Priests*, p. 20.

[3] Fulton Sheen, quoted in the *National Catholic Reporter*, February 1, 1967.

[4] *TIC*, p. 176.

duction of a process of preparation for candidates for the sacrament of Confirmation. Candidates would receive the sacrament in high school after "liturgical and spiritual training of two or three years duration."[5] Initially, this idea was rejected and even frowned upon because the practice had always been to administer the sacrament of Confirmation at a much younger age, but Sheen lived to see other dioceses implement his program.[6]

It has been said that the seminary in a diocese is its heart. The diocese of Rochester had its own seminary which at the time of Sheen's installation not only educated its own future priests but those of about one dozen other dioceses. Sheen always felt it a great privilege to ordain priests for the missions. Now, as ordinary of a diocese, he would ordain men to serve in a diocese of which he was bishop. However, his first ordination as Ordinary was for a religious order. On March 16, 1967, Andrew Apostoli, now a member of the Franciscan Friars of the Renewal, was the first man ordained to the priesthood by Sheen in the diocese of Rochester. Father Apostoli recalls Sheen having told him and others that while Rome had offered him two archdioceses and five dioceses, he asked for the diocese of Rochester because of its reputation for good priests. Father Apostoli recalled that his day of ordination was a very special day for two reasons. Primarily because he was going to become a priest, but also because he felt it a special blessing that he would be ordained by Sheen. Father Apostoli recalls Sheen saying to him at his ordination that the reforms of the Second Vatican Council would only be successful if there was a renewal of the priesthood and the renewal had to be based on faithfulness. He also

---

[5] "Awaiting Confirmation," *Newsweek*, February 27, 1967.
[6] *Newsweek*, February 27, 1967.

expressed regrets that while Apostoli had received the power of the Holy Spirit at his ordination, he was finishing four years of theology without ever having made a study of the Third Person of the Holy Trinity.[7] Sheen's words left a strong impression upon Father Apostoli, particularly what he said concerning the Holy Spirit. Apostoli later began preaching retreats to priests. The theme of his first retreat was "The Holy Spirit in the Life of a Priest." The retreat inspired him to write about the Holy Spirit, not only for priests but for religious and laity as well.[8]

Sheen was also disturbed by the fact that many seminaries were instituting a curriculum that placed less emphasis on the doctrinal and the spiritual and more on the sociological. This new emphasis had developed during the turmoil that engulfed society during the 1960's and 1970's and resulted in a dissolution or dichotomy between the priesthood and the *victimhood* or co-redemptive aspect of the priest's role and relationship with Christ.

Sheen resolved that his seminarians' education would be well-rounded. He invited professors from Europe to teach at the seminary, one of whom was the Reverend Michael Bourdeaux, whose specialty was Religion in Eastern Europe. Sheen issued the invitation with the specific intention of edu-

---

[7] In the course of my research at the Sheen Archives, I came across a typescript of possibly the last written work of Sheen. The typescript is entitled: "The Holy Spirit Illuminating Minds." The typescript totals some six pages, including an introductory page and a chapter titled: "The Holy Spirit in Relation to the Head and to the Body." The present director of the Fulton Sheen Archives, Father William Graff, believes that these pages were part of a book on the Holy Spirit that Sheen was writing at the time of his death.

[8] Father Andrew Apostoli C.F.R., interviewed by author in New York City on September 26, 1999. He is the author of three books published by Alba House on the Holy Spirit and one published by Pauline Books and Media on celibacy. They are: *The Gift of God, The Holy Spirit* (1994); *The Comforter, The Spirit of Joy* (1995); *The Advocate, The Holy Spirit* (1999), and *When God Asks For An Undivided Heart* (1995).

cating the seminarians about the sufferings that Christians were enduring because of their Catholic faith. Dr. Douglas Hyde, the ex-Communist editor of the *London Daily Worker* and convert was invited by Sheen to teach techniques in dealing with converts. What Hyde had once used well to "convert" people to Communism, he now was teaching to bring people to the Gospel.

Sheen drew the attention of the nation when, on July 30, 1967, from Sacred Heart Cathedral, Sheen became the first United States bishop to call for the unconditional withdrawal of American armed forces from Vietnam, a call which he withdrew two years later stating that his position was no longer applicable. Sheen's call was in conflict with the position of Cardinal Spellman and other members of the hierarchy who supported America's involvement in the war.[9] Sheen, at first, believed that the cost of the war, both economically and spiritually, was too high, "Better to use the money to alleviate the sufferings of the poor."[10] According to Sheen, the United States should "take the moral high ground and show our power by appreciating the weak."[11] Sheen's call for an end to the war was in accord with Pope Paul VI's demand in a speech at the United Nations: "War! War, never again!"

Sheen's concern for the poor led to what was called, "The St. Bridget's Affair." It turned out to be the defining moment and turning point for him as Bishop of Rochester. He proposed turning over the structures and land of St. Bridget's, one square block in the inner city with about one hundred parishioners, to the Federal government. The land would be used to build

---

[9] *Newsweek*, August 16, 1967.

[10] Fulton Sheen, quoted in *The New York Times*, October 29, 1969.

[11] D.P. Noonan, *The Passion of Fulton Sheen*, Our Sunday Visitor, Huntington, IN, 1975, pp. 28-29.

affordable housing for the poor. The idea had merit, but the consensus was that Sheen had gone about it the wrong way. When the proposal was announced on Ash Wednesday, February 29, 1968, the reaction was swift, and for the most part, negative. The pastor, Father Francis H. Vogt, and the parishioners were not consulted, which was seen as inconsistent, considering Sheen's new "democratic" style of consultation. Evidently, the great communicator failed to communicate. But Sheen countered that only a few were consulted in secret about the proposal at the request of the government. The local press, parishioners and clergy all protested against the offer, basically because of the manner in which it was accomplished.[12] The local press was outraged that they were informed after the national media; the parishioners were upset at the thought of losing their parish; and the clergy thought that other ways could be found to help the poor besides giving away church property.[13] Sheen received a petition from a number of the priests of the diocese asking that he withdraw the offer. He was surprised at the level of opposition and believed much of it was artificially stimulated. College students traveled to the Pastoral Office with signs condemning him personally. When visiting a school, he was confronted by several hundred people protesting his decision. Some in the crowd picked up pebbles and threw them at his car. The uproar and the protests, particularly from some of the clergy, led him to withdraw the offer four days after it was made. After withdrawing the offer, the petition to Sheen, which he was told would remain private, was leaked to the press.

In 1969, Sheen would reach his seventy-fifth birthday, the age for retirement for bishops, as recently decreed by the Coun-

---

[12] *Ibid.*, p. 142.
[13] *TIC*, p. 180.

cil. So, in the spring of 1969, at a private audience, Sheen offered his resignation as bishop to Pope Paul VI. Sheen had to bring up his retirement several times in his meetings with the Pope. Finally, Sheen said to the Pope: "Your Holiness, you have not answered my question. Will you graciously accept my resignation as Bishop of Rochester since I have reached the age limit to be an active bishop?" In October of 1969, Sheen's resignation was accepted by the Pope.[14] The St. Bridget's Affair left its mark on him. As one observer noted: "Disheartened and profoundly saddened by the St. Bridget's episode, he never fully recovered, and left Rochester with his first real taste of failure."[15]

His brief tenure as Bishop of Rochester could truly be said to have been his Calvary. In 1979, Sheen recounts in his autobiography the following, "That empty church (St. Bridget's), rectory, and school stand abandoned today in the inner city, a monument to my failure to do anything about it." Less than twenty years later, in July of 1997, St. Bridget's Parish was closed and the less than 100 parishioners were informed that they would be welcome in a nearby parish. The rectory had been closed some years earlier because there were no monies available to pay for needed repairs. In 1969 Sheen offered the following impression in an interview in *The New York Times* about his years in Rochester:

> I was too young for the old ones — by demanding that
> we introduce the innovations called for by the Second
> Vatican Council, and too old for the young ones — they

---

[14] *Ibid.*, p. 239.

[15] Kathleen Riley Fields, "Fulton J. Sheen: An American Catholic Response to the Twentieth Century," dissertation, Notre Dame University, South Bend, IN, 1989, p. 507.

didn't want advanced ideas to come from my generation.[16]

Time wrote that Sheen "never seemed an appropriate choice to head the diocese of Rochester."[17] *The National Catholic Reporter* wrote that he was "great at getting an idea but not at carrying it through."[18] Douglas Roche offered a more favorable view of Sheen:

> The ecumenical movement blessed by Vatican II went forward in Rochester by leaps and bounds…. In every action that he took, Sheen revealed an intense commitment to conciliar thought as formulated in the Council documents…. The conciliar revolution, launched by Pope John was brought down to earth and planted in local soil by Fulton Sheen.[19]

Concerning retirement, Sheen, said; "When I resigned, I did not 'retire,' I *retreaded*. I took on another kind of work. I believe that we spend our last days very much the way we lived…. I believe that we can somehow or other work up until the last day God draws the line and says: 'Now it is finished.'"[20] One of Sheen's greatest joys and one which he continued to do while his health allowed, was give retreats.

> If I were asked which of the many activities of my life outside of the eminently priestly privileges such as offering the Eucharist, appealed to me the most, I could

---

[16] *New York Times*, November 30, 1969. Sheen made similar remarks in *TIC*, also see D.P. Noonan's, *The Passion of Fulton Sheen*, p. 146.

[17] *Time*, October 29, 1969.

[18] *National Catholic Reporter*, October 29, 1969.

[19] Douglas J. Roche, *The Catholic Revolution*, David McKay Co., New York, 1968, pp. 70 and 79.

[20] *TIC*, p. 183.

not answer. I have loved every work to which I have been called or sent. But perhaps the most meaningful and gratifying experience of my life has been giving retreats to priests, not only because they brought me into contact with the priesthood, but because the very review one makes of his own spiritual life in order to speak to others helps oneself, too. I really wonder if the priests that made these retreats received as much from me as I did from them.[21]

---

[21] *Ibid.*, pp. 215-216.

15

The Priesthood

THIS BOOK BEGAN WITH A STATEMENT BY SHEEN THAT HE ESSENTIALLY saw his life as that of being a priest and that he can never remember a time in his life when he did not want to be a priest. As a young boy living and working on his parents' farm, he realized early on that he was not cut out to be a farmer. His prayer to God that he might receive the vocation to be a priest was the Rosary. The Rosary became a component of his prayers early on because it was prayed together by his family every night before retiring. Sheen recalled that his family never spoke of his becoming a priest but when he informed his parents that he wanted to enter the seminary they admitted: "We always prayed that you might become a priest," and "if it is your vocation, be a good one."[1] Sheen did not talk about his desire to anyone (except Father Kelly, a priest at the cathedral parish) because he believed that a vocation to the priesthood is very sacred.

Sheen believed that most vocations to the priesthood happen through a "silent but insistent whisper." It is a whisper that demands a response. A man can either accept or reject the call but if it is accepted, Sheen states it must be made in willing obedience. Sheen was willing to answer the call but he was

---

[1] *TIC*, p. 30.

initially hesitant. Not because of any problem with the life of a priest, but because he believed himself unworthy.

It was because of the interest and words of a priest friend that Sheen entered the seminary. Sheen related what happened. After receiving a scholarship to college, Sheen wanted to tell Father Bergin who had befriended him. After excitedly telling Father Bergin, the priest responded by placing his hands on the shoulders of Sheen. He looked him straight in the eye and asked him: "Do you believe in God?" Sheen responded that he did. "I mean *practically*, not from a theoretical point of view," said the priest. "Well, I hope I do," said Sheen. Father Bergin asserted, "You know you have a vocation; you should be going to the seminary." Sheen countered that he had received a wonderful scholarship to college and he would very much like to have a good education. The priest insisted: "Tear up the scholarship; go to the seminary. That is what the Lord wants you to do. And if you do it, trusting in Him, you will receive a far better university education after you are ordained than before." Sheen tore up the scholarship and entered the seminary, never regretting his decision. The visit with his priest friend proved to be prophetic for he did, indeed, receive a far better university education after he was ordained than he could ever have received had he accepted the scholarship which he was offered.

Sheen believed that vocations are a gift to be treasured and that "there are many more vocations to the priesthood than those which result in Ordination, as there are more seeds planted than those which bear fruit." He agreed with St. Thomas that God gives the Church a suitable number of vocations, "provided the unworthy ones are dismissed and the worthy ones are well trained."[2] Sheen often expressed the belief that it is the responsibility, even the obligation, of the priest who, while

---

2 *Ibid.*, p. 35.

he cannot impart a vocation, can certainly promote a vocation to the priesthood: "On the last day, God will ask us priests: Where are your children? How many vocations have you fostered?" Sheen relates the following story concerning a boy he "intuitively" thought had a vocation.

> I left my dinner and went out of the hotel to the boy and asked him where he went to school. He told me that he was going to a public school. I said: "With a name like that (his name was Irish), why don't you go to a Catholic school?" He said: "I got kicked out." "Who kicked you out?" I asked. "The pastor and the Mother Superior of the school." I promised: "I will get you back in." He asked who I was but I responded that I couldn't tell him. He then remarked: "No, they said nobody could ever get me back into a Catholic school; I will never be allowed to return." I went to see the pastor and the Mother Superior of the school and I told them: "I know of three boys who were thrown out of religious schools: one because he was constantly drawing pictures during geography class; another because he was fond of fighting; and the third because he kept revolutionary books hidden under a mattress. No one knows the valedictorians of those classes, but the first boy was Hitler, the second Mussolini and the third Stalin. I am sure that if the superiors of those schools had given those boys another chance, they might have turned out differently in the world. Maybe this boy will prove himself worthy if you take him back."

As Sheen tells it, the boy was allowed to return and became a missionary among the Eskimos. Many voices are heard today questioning the Church's practice of demanding celibacy on the part of its priests. It is felt in some quarters that it is too hard a life. After all, the Scriptures say that it is not good for man to be alone. And wouldn't doing away with the celibacy requirement solve the vocation shortage? Sheen looked upon celibacy as not something that one gives to the Church but rather something a priest *receives*, "very much as a girl may receive a proposal."[3] He believed that celibacy is a gift. One is free to accept or reject it. It is not something that is forced on a person. Rather, it is something that is proposed. It is only for those to whom it is granted, "Let anyone accept this who can." He explained celibacy as a passionless passion, a wild tranquility and that, while both marriage and celibacy are good, they are complimentary, not competitive. The difference, Sheen maintained, is that celibacy belongs more to the next world while marriage belongs more to this. As this world shall pass away, so shall marriage. As Jesus said, "In the Kingdom of Heaven there is no marriage or giving in marriage." The celibate is called to work for the kingdom of God, begetting spiritual children, while those in the married state beget children through the uniting of two into one flesh. Ideally, both want God, but journey to Him under different conditions. Sheen admitted that there were difficulties inherent to the celibate life but responded that the initiative is on God's side and the response is on ours. Just as anything with God as its aim can only be attained with His grace, so too the celibate can live out the life *he* has chosen if he relies on God. Jesus spoke to His apostles about the life of the eunuchs who made themselves so for the kingdom of God: "Though this is impossible with men, it is not impossible with God." Sheen added that when one loves Christ, celibacy, if chosen, is no burden. Only when one falls out of love with Christ, does it become one. When approached from the vantage point of love, this law of the Church, while remaining hard, is bearable and joyful.

---

[3] *Ibid.*, p. 204.

When Sheen was asked if he lived the life of a good priest, he responded: "When I compare myself with missionaries who have become dry martyrs by leaving their own country and family to teach other peoples, when I think of the sufferings of my brother-priests in Eastern Europe, when I look at the saintly faces of some of my brother-priests in monasteries and in the missions, and the beautiful resignation of priests in hospitals who suffer from cancer, and when I just even look at my many brothers in Christ whom I admire so much, I say: 'No, I have not been the kind of priest I should have been or would have liked to have been.'" While Sheen is a bit harsh in self-assessment, he had a discipline that he believed helped him accomplish much in his chosen vocation.

There was one hour in each day that Sheen referred to as "The Hour that makes my day." One cannot discuss Sheen and the priesthood without referring to that hour which was so central to his life. On the day of his ordination, Sheen resolved to spend a continuous Holy Hour in the presence of the Blessed Sacrament every day. It was a promise that he kept all his life. The practice of making a Holy Hour began a year before his ordination at St. Paul's Seminary. The purpose of the Holy Hour, was to encourage the individual to a deep encounter with Christ. It is one thing to know *about* Christ, it is quite another to *know* Christ, and the only way to know Christ is through prayer. This is especially true for the priest, who is called to be what Sheen refers to as a "Little Jesus." He pointed out that with anything new in life there is initially an entire giving of self to that newness. Upon ordination, a priest is set on giving himself entirely to Christ. As with every earthly thing, however, the exhilaration soon wears off, the honeymoon ends. The exhilaration at being called "Father" leaves. But, it doesn't have to be that way.

Sheen's own personal prayer life, while rooted in the Divine Presence in the Eucharist, needed to be cultivated. For true prayer to occur, one has to be available and open to the prompting of the Spirit: "We do not say: 'Listen, Lord, for Thy servant speaks,' but 'Speak, Lord, for thy servant heareth.'"[4] This openness to a personal encounter with Christ does not happen overnight nor does a response come necessarily within a specific time frame. One moves on, throwing oneself into one's work and responsibilities. Thus the excuse: "I do not have the time for prayer." Pope John Paul II has said that time with Christ is never time wasted. Sheen wholeheartedly would agree. He described sitting before the Blessed Sacrament as "like a body exposing itself before the sun to absorb the rays." Any sun bather knows that to achieve a nice tan takes time but with patient endurance it happens.

Sheen believed that it was very important for priests to prepare their sermons well: "All my sermons are prepared in front of the Blessed Sacrament. As recreation was most pleasant and profitable in the sun, so homiletic creativity is best nourished before the Eucharist. The most brilliant ideas come from meeting God face to face."[5]

Sheen does not hesitate to state that it was the Holy Hour that helped him sustain his vocation. He warns priests that a failure to love the Eucharist will lead to eventual decline as a priest. This judgment of Sheen's is based on the fall of Judas as recorded in the Scriptures at the end of the sixth chapter of John. The fall of Judas began and ended around the Eucharist. Jesus unveils the Eucharist and foretells that someone would betray Him. People believe that Judas fell because he loved money. Sheen felt that this was not the case, stating that the history of the Church shows that many who love money remain in the

---

[4] *Ibid.*, p. 191.
[5] *Ibid.*, p. 75.

Church. Judas fell because he didn't believe. He was, as Sheen states an "Anti-Eucharist Priest."[6] Sheen posits that there are twelve types of priests. One for every apostle first called by Him. He describes priests who are lukewarm about the Real Presence as a "type" of Judas who worked miracles and preached with the other apostles, but when the Lord announced the Eucharist, secretly resolved to leave. The Lord knew it and said, "Have I not chosen you, all twelve. Yet one of you is a devil" (Jn 6:71). But Judas stayed with Christ for almost two more years. It was at the Last Supper, the night Jesus gave us the Eucharist that he finally broke, "The devil had put into the mind of Judas, son of Simon Iscariot, to betray Him" (Jn 13:2). "Alas for that man by whom he is betrayed" (Lk 22:22; Ac 1:18). He described the lukewarm priest as follows: "Seemingly had faith for the time he spent with his clerical brethren. But refused ever to attend a Holy Hour. Was against keeping the Blessed Sacrament in the Church; reserved it in a small room off the office. Ridiculed Benediction and Eucharistic devotions; really had no faith but never gave any indications that he would leave the Church until the bishop held a Eucharistic Congress. Then he left and never came back."

Sheen believed the Eucharist is essential to our "one-ness" with Christ and is a test to the fidelity of His followers: "First, He lost the masses, for it was too hard a saying and they no longer followed Him. Secondly, He lost some of His disciples: 'They walked with Him no more.' Third, it split His apostolic band, for Judas is here announced as the betrayer."

Sheen believed it was the Holy Hour, aside from its spiritual benefits that kept his feet from wandering too far:

---

6 Sheen, *Those Mysterious Priests*, Doubleday & Co., Garden City, NY, 1974, p. 193.

Being tethered to a tabernacle, one's rope for finding other pastures is not so long. That dim tabernacle lamp, however pale and faint, had some mysterious luminosity to darken the brightness of 'bright lights.' The Holy Hour became like an oxygen tank to revive the breadth of the Holy Spirit in the midst of the foul and fetid atmosphere of the world. Even when it seemed so unprofitable and lacking in spiritual intimacy, I still had the sensation of being at least like a dog at the master's door, ready in case he called me. The Hour, too, became a magister and teacher, for although before we love anyone we must have a knowledge of that person, nevertheless, *after* we know, it is love that increases knowledge. Theological insights are gained not only from the two covers of a treatise, but from two knees on a priedieu before a tabernacle.[7]

As to what a priest is called to be, Sheen defers to the laity: "The laity see the priest as he really is supposed to be — 'another Christ.'"[8] While a priest should bear this in mind, Sheen exhorted both priest and laity to realize that while:

We have the awesome power to act *in Persona Christi*, that is, to forgive the grossest of sins, to transplant the Cross of Calvary to the altar, to give divine birth to thousands of children at the baptismal font, and to usher souls on deathbeds to the Kingdom of Heaven. But, on the other hand, we look like anyone else. We have the same weaknesses as other men, some to the bottle, or a woman, or a dollar, or a desire to be a little higher in the hierarchy of power. Each priest is a man with a body of soft clay. To keep that treasure pure, he

---

[7] *TIC*, pp. 192, 194.

[8] *Ibid.*, p. 5.

has to be stretched out on a cross of fire. Our fall can
be greater than the fall of anyone else because of the
height from which we tumble. Of all the bad men, bad
religious men are the worst, because they were called
to be closer to Christ.[9]

Sheen does not say that it is necessary for everyone to follow his custom of a daily Holy Hour but he does suggest that
if one wishes to truly attain a relationship with the Lord, and
not just know *about* Jesus but *know* Jesus, then the Holy Hour
is a sure means toward that end. Sheen recognized that most
do not have the practice of making a Holy Hour and is "abso-
lutely sure that, in the sight of God, they are a thousand times
more worthy." Yet, for him it was his way of, as he describes it,
keeping in step with his brother priests in the service of the
Lord.

---

[9] *Ibid.*, p. 4.

16

The Woman Sheen Loved

WHEN I WAS BAPTIZED AS AN INFANT, MY MOTHER LAID me on the altar of the Blessed Mother in Saint Mary's Church in El Paso, Illinois, and consecrated me to her. As an infant may be unconscious of a birthmark, so was I unconscious of the dedication... but the mark was always there. Like a piece of iron to a magnet, I was drawn to her before I knew her, but never drawn to her without Christ.[1]

Next to his desire of exposing the world to the dangers of Communism and the salvation of souls, was his conviction of the importance of Mary, the Mother of God in Salvation History. One of *the* major influences on Sheen was Mary, the Mother of Jesus. He offered Mass on Saturdays to her.[2] As to why this was his practice, Sheen says: "When I was ordained, I took a resolution to offer the Holy Sacrifice of the Eucharist every Saturday to the Blessed Mother, renewing my feeble love of her and invoking her intercession. All this makes me very certain that when I go before the Judgment Seat of Christ, He will say to me in His Mercy: 'I heard My Mother speak of you.'" As writer Kathleen Riley Fields notes, Sheen dedicated all his pubished works to Mary and often visited her shrines.

---

[1] Sheen, *TIC*, p. 316.

[2] *Ibid.,* p. 317.

The more private side of Fulton Sheen, attested to by those who knew him well, was his intense spirituality and devotion. His spirituality never wavered, and he credited it as the sustaining source of his strength. The same man who loved the adulation of the crowds and the trappings of celebrity spent an hour every day in quiet prayer and meditation, the hour that made his day. Equally intense was his devotion to the Blessed Virgin, manifest in so many ways. The piety of Fulton Sheen caused him to dedicate every book he wrote to her, to make a pilgrimage to Lourdes or Fatima during every trip to Europe.[3]

Sheen believed that it was not enough for him to have a particular devotion to Mary, as her Son's priest, but that he was to use his abilities to make her known and loved.

Sheen's devotion to Mary began in the home where he was raised. The family would gather together each evening, as mentioned earlier, to pray the Rosary. Later, as a student at Saint Viator's College and Seminary in Minnesota, just before dinner, Sheen would lead the other students in the recitation of the Rosary. Sheen was the first student to do so. It had always been reserved to one of the priests, but "Sheen's voice and presence had by that time already developed to the point where he could be heard — sans mike — all over the football field."[4]

As we saw earlier, Sheen became a master of the radio and television mediums. Before each radio program, which ran for twenty-two years, Sheen would dedicate his program to the Blessed Mother at St. Patrick's Cathedral, which was located

---

[3]   Kathleeen Riley Fields, "Fulton J. Sheen: An American Catholic Response to the Twentieth Century, " dissertation. Notre Dame University, South Bend, Indiana, 1989, p. 512.

[4]   *Ibid.*, p. 22.

across from the broadcasting studio.[5] As a television evangelist, the studio set where Sheen's show *Life Is Worth Living* was
broadcast, had only two props: a blackboard and a statue of the
Blessed Virgin Mary, which Sheen named "Our Lady of Television." Sheen received many requests for copies of the statue
and used the monies raised from sales of the statue for "the poor
of the world" to be distributed through the Society for the
Propagation of the Faith.[6] The book, published with the same
title as his television series, was dedicated by Sheen: "To our
Heavenly Mother who stands behind me at every telecast and
before whom I kneel in filial love, that these words borne on
waves of light may bring readers to the Word and Light of the
World."[7]

While at the offices at the Society for the Propagation of
the Faith, Sheen would lead the staff and visitors in the Rosary
every day. Florence Lee was Bishop Sheen's secretary during
all his years at the Propagation of the Faith, and worked very
closely with him. She recounts the following: "The whole staff
would gather, at mid-afternoon, to pray the Rosary as well as
to spend fifteen minutes reflecting upon the Scriptures. It was
really a family affair. All visitors were invited to join us. Bishop
Sheen would lead us in prayer. For all of us it was the highlight of the day." Miss Lee also noted that "Bishop Sheen's first
Episcopal ring was purchased at Lourdes, where he had an image of the Blessed Mother imprinted upon it." She went on to
state that, "The ring was replaced with another ring that all the
bishops present at the Council (Second Vatican) received from
Pope Paul VI." Through the years it became apparent to those

---

[5] John Jay Daly, "The Man Behind the Mike," *The Sign*, May, 1945, p. 511.

[6] *Mission* magazine, January/February, 1953.

[7] Sheen, *Life is Worth Living*, McGraw-Hill Book Co., New York, 1953.

who worked with Sheen, as well as those who knew him, Mary was an integral part of his day.[8]

As related earlier, Sheen prayed through the intercession of Mary, that he might be named a bishop.[9] He chose the following as his Episcopal motto: *"Da Per Matrem Me Venire"* translated as: "Grant that I may come to You through Your Mother." Following his ordination as Bishop, Sheen had an audience with Pope Pius XII. Afterward Sheen "flew, almost at once, to Lourdes for his twenty-third visit to the grotto, the spot on earth which was probably closest to his heart."[10]

Sheen had no hesitation to ask others to pray to Mary for him. At his installation at Sacred Heart Cathedral as Bishop of Rochester, on December 15, 1966, Sheen asked his congregation to: "Pray for me daily to Mary, my patroness, that as she formed Jesus physically in her body, so may she form Jesus mystically in my soul, the better to serve you with a passionless passion and wild tranquility."[11]

Sheen characterizes his devotion to the Blessed Mother as having brought him to the discovery of a new dimension of the sacredness of suffering: "If Christ the Lord had summoned His Mother, who was free from sin, to share His Cross, then the Christian must scratch from his vocabulary the word 'deserve.'" This "discovery" on the part of Sheen was made when he spent four months in a hospital after he had open-heart surgery. He believed that it was during this period that he realized as never

---

[8] Interview by author with Miss Florence Lee, in November 1997. Miss Lee recently retired as secretary to Bishop William McCormack, present National Director of the Society for the Propagation of the Faith.

[9] See page 83.

[10] Gretta Palmer, "Bishop Fulton J. Sheen," *The Catholic Digest*, October, 1951, p. 59. Sheen stated in 1979 that he made about thirty pilgrimages to the shrine of Our Lady of Lourdes and about ten to her shrine at Fatima. See also *TIC*, p. 317.

[11] A copy of his sermon can be found at the Fulton Sheen Archives.

before, the greatest gift the Lord might have given to him was "His summons to the Cross… where I found His continuing self-disclosure."[12] He also discovered that

> the Blessed Mother not only gives sweets, but she also gives bitter medicine. Too striking to be missed was that on three feast days of Our Lady I was brought to the door of death, and endured great suffering. The first was on the Feast of Our Lady of Mount Carmel, July 16, when the doctors stayed with me all day and night trying to preserve the small flickering spark of life. Then came another operation on the Feast of the Assumption, August 15, and the implanting of a pacemaker. By this time I was beginning to feel a kind of holy dread of what might happen on September 8, when the Church celebrates her birthday. Sure enough, a kidney infection developed which, over a period of several weeks, made me feel some new tortures.[13]

Sheen believed that Mary was uniting him with suffering in imitation of her Son who "even paid in advance for her gift in being immaculately conceived," and because of her maternal love for him as Mother of the Priesthood.[14]

> As I reflected on this concomitance of the Church festivals of Mary and my enforced solidarity with the Cross, I took it as a sign of the special predilection of Mary. If the Lord who called her, who "deserved" no pain, to stand at the foot of the Cross, why should He not call me? If I had expressed a love for her as Mother

---

[12] *TIC*, p. 350.

[13] *Ibid.*, pp. 322-323.

[14] *Ibid.* Sheen is referring here to the foreseen merits of Christ obtained for mankind through his passion and death on Calvary.

of the Priesthood, why should she not, in maternal love, make me more like her Son by forcing me to become a victim. If my own earthly mother laid me on her altar at birth, why should not my Heavenly Mother lay me at His Cross as I come to the end of my life.[15]

Mary, as mother, protects all her sons and daughters. Sheen was convinced that Mary loved him as she loves all those who love her Son. Because Mary is our mother, we are her children. Just as the Lord instructed us that we are to be like little children if we wish to enter into His kingdom, Sheen believed that our devotion to Mary must be childlike as well. Thus, Sheen often ended his sermons and lectures reciting a poem that for many became synonymous with him. His rendition of the poem "Lovely Lady Dressed in Blue" left such an impression, that I found those who knew him or those who had memories of him, would spontaneously begin to recite a few lines themselves. The poem reflects Sheen's child-like faith that Mary can show us the way, a faith Sheen desired to share with all.

> Lovely Lady dressed in blue —
> teach me how to pray!
> God was just your little Boy,
> tell me what to say!
> Did you lift Him up, sometimes,
> gently on your knee?
> Did you sing to Him the way
> Mother does to me?
> Did you hold his hand at night?
> Did you ever try
> telling stories of the world?

---

[15] *Ibid.*

O! And did He cry?
Do you really think He cares
if I tell Him things —
Little things that happen? And
do Angel's wings
make a noise? And can He hear
me if I speak low?
Does He understand me now?
Tell me for you know!
Lovely Lady dressed in blue,
teach me how to pray!
God was just your little Boy
and, you know the way.[16]

[16] "To Our Lady." From *The Child on His Knees* by Mary Dixon Thayer. Copyright 1926 by Macmillan Publishing Co., Inc., renewed 1954 by Mary D.T. Fremont Smith.

17

The Remaining Years

S HORTLY FOLLOWING HIS RESIGNATION AS BISHOP OF ROCHESTER, Sheen returned to the medium that had made him a household name. He made an appearance on the CBS television show *60 Minutes*, and was interviewed by Mike Wallace. Wallace asked Sheen why it was that he did not go higher in the Church, to which Sheen responded, "It is possible for a man in the Church to go up and up, and I would have gone higher and higher… but I refused to pay the price." Wallace inquired, "And what would that be?" "Well, I felt it would be disloyalty to my own principles, and I think to the Christian practice." Sheen once said that attacks against the Church hurt him as attacks against his own mother would. Remaining true to those Christian principles, not seeking to cause any individual or institution harm, Sheen never addressed the particulars of just what he meant by his statement on television. This is consistent with a statement he made in 1955 concerning scandal.

> The fondness of the twentieth century for scandal is due to a great extent to its guilty conscience. By finding others' skirts stained with mud, some rejoice that their dusty and ragged ones are not so bad after all.[1]

---

[1] Sheen, *Way to Inner Peace*, p. 39.

The sufferings that Pope John XXIII referred to at Sheen's audience with him are known by a few. Many expected, some hoped, that Sheen would address those "sufferings" or grievances by doing a "tell-all" on *60 Minutes* or at least set the record straight in his autobiography. Sheen tells why he chose not to:

> The curious would like me to open healed wounds; the media, in particular, would relish a chapter which would pass judgment on others, particularly because, as a French author expressed it: *nous vivons aux temps des assassins* — "we live in the days of assassins" — where evil is sought in lives more than good in order to justify a world with a bad conscience... silence is recommended because any discussion of conflicts within the Church diminishes the content of the Christ-love within the Mystical Body — as the hand excessively rubbing the eye diminishes vision. Impatience and blame is a blight to humanity; rebellion against having one's own will crossed is a plague to obedience. If we are right in a conflict the Lord bids us to absorb any wrongs like a sponge; if we are wrong, we are to see others as the instrument of working His Will. A dog when it is struck with a stick bites the stick, not discerning that the stick only moves as the hand directs it. The dog never learns the lesson and most of us never learn it until the end of life. Silence is recommended because if I judge not, I will not be judged. As we hope the Good Lord will throw our sins in the wastebasket, may He not justly expect that we throw our self-righteousness into it also. As the prophet observed: we receive fewer blows than we deserve, for "Our God has punished us less than our iniquities deserve."[2]

---

[2]   *TIC*, pp. 310-314.

Sheen believed that any sufferings that he received at the hands of others were a punishment for his sins: "In punishing us for our sins, God often mercifully uses gloves, that is, human instruments. He does not use His bare hand; the penalty would be too great. The less we connect the Providence of God with all that happens, the more we are upset with the smallest annoyances of daily life." He is certain that God, as he puts it, "made certain people throw stones at me." But he is certain of one other thing as well: "I have thrown stones at other people, and for those stonings I beg His mercy and pardon."

Fulton J. Sheen's remaining years would be active ones, living out his chosen vocation as he always had — serving the Church. The number of speaking engagements were not as many but he did continue to give priest retreats. In 1966, Sheen was elected, by the American Episcopacy, Chairman of the Committee for the Propagation of the Faith as well as being appointed to the Administrative Board of the National Council of Catholic Bishops. In 1969, he was appointed by Pope Paul VI to the Papal Commission for Nonbelievers and named Archbishop of the Titular See of Newport, Wales.

It was Sheen's desire that he die in the presence of the Blessed Sacrament and on a Saturday or Marian Feast Day. This desire of his was based upon two resolutions that he made many years earlier: "On the day of my ordination, I made two resolutions. One, I would offer the Holy Eucharist every Saturday in honor of the Blessed Mother to solicit her protection on my priesthood. Two, I resolved also to spend a continuous Holy Hour every day in the presence of Our Lord in the Blessed Sacrament. In the course of my priesthood I have kept both of these resolutions." Bishop Sheen's practice of dedicating his Mass on Saturday to honor the Blessed Mother is based upon tradition: "The practice of dedicating Saturday to Mary is very old and is based upon a legendary yet substantially accurate account. On the Saturday after Christ's death and His disciples' abandonment of Him, Mary was the only one to preserve intact her faith in the Divinity of her Son. As a result she merited to receive an exceptional appearance of Jesus on *that day*. Saturday is dedicated to Mary by a Mass or Office of the Blessed Virgin Mary."[3]

Because of Sheen's belief in the importance and legitimacy of the Papacy, one could say that the apex of Sheen's life occurred in 1979 on October 2nd at St. Patrick's Cathedral. Pope John Paul II was making his first visit to the United States as Pope. Upon entering the sanctuary with Terence Cardinal Cooke, the Holy Father asked for Archbishop Sheen. Sheen was off to the side and behind the main altar and had to be found. An assistant to the Cardinal brought Sheen to the Pope. The Holy Father embraced him to thunderous applause from the audience. The Pope told him, "You have written and spoken well of the Lord Jesus and you are a loyal son of the Church."[4]

For many years, at St. Agnes Church in Manhattan, New York, Sheen gave a meditation on Good Friday, on the *Seven Last Words of Christ*. Loudspeakers had to be placed up and down the streets so the overflow crowds could hear him. In memory of Fulton Sheen, the street on which the Church is located, in midtown Manhattan, was named by Edward Koch, then Mayor of New York, "Fulton Sheen Place," on October 7, 1980.

---

[3] *Ibid.*, p. 187. "Through these liturgical acts, Christians exalt the person of Mary in the action that renews the sacrifice of Christ and in the action that prolongs His prayer. The liturgical reform of Vatican II did not abolish this traditional practice." See Anthony Buono, "Saturday of Our Lady," in *Dictionary of Mary*, Catholic Book Publishing, New York, 1985, pp. 306-307.

[4] Interview by author with Monsignor Eugene Clarke, Pastor of St. Agnes Church, New York in November 1997. Monsignor Clarke was secretary to Cardinal Cooke at the time of the Pope's visit.

Just five weeks after his meeting with the Pope, Sheen died at home in the presence of the Blessed Sacrament as had always been his wish. At Sheen's funeral, the late Archbishop Edward T. O'Meara, who had succeeded him as National Director of the Propagation of the Faith and a close friend, spoke these words during his homily:

> Frequently he spoke of his death and to the amazement and oftentimes the consternation of his hearers and friends. But he said: "It is not that I do not love life; I do. It is just that I want to see the Lord. I have spent many hours before Him in the Blessed Sacrament. I have spoken to Him in prayer, and about Him to everyone who would listen, and now I want to see him face to face." ... A voice is silent in the midst of the Church and in our land, the like of which will not be heard again in our day. The vocation of Fulton Sheen is consummated; he has responded with one final "yes" to the call of God, a "yes" so final that human frailty and infirmity can never reverse it. Dear friend, Archbishop Sheen, we are all the better because you were in our midst and were our friend. We trust you to the care of your "Lovely Lady dressed in blue."[5]

With thousands of people, and cardinals, bishops and priests from all over the world in attendance, Sheen was laid to rest in the burial vault beneath the high altar of St. Patrick's Cathedral. Monsignor John Tracy Ellis put it so well when he said, "It was altogether appropriate that this is his final resting

---

5 Edward T. O'Meara, "Bye now Fulton Sheen, and God Love You Forever"; homily delivered at St. Patrick's Cathedral on December 13, 1979. Copies can be found at the Fulton Sheen Archives and it is also included in the Epilogue in *TIC*, p. 351.

place, for the pulpit of that historic Church had never been so frequently and so uniquely adorned as it had by the Twentieth Century's most famous Catholic preacher."[6]

---

[6]   John Tracy Ellis, *Catholic Bishops: A Memoir*, Michael Glazier, Inc., Wilmington, DE, 1983, p. 84.

18

Conclusion

A ND WHEN THE BABE GREW IN GRACE AND WISDOM, HE went into the public lanes and market places, and began to teach a new doctrine to men — the doctrine of the Divine Sense of Humor. Everything he said, everything he did could be summed up in these words: *Nothing in this world is to be taken seriously, nothing* — except the salvation of a soul. 'What shall it profit a man, if he gain the whole world, and suffer the loss of his soul?' The world, and the things that are in it, will one day, like an Arab's tent, be folded away. There is nothing that endures but God![1]

These pages began with Archbishop Sheen stating that he saw his life as that of a priest. From an early age he wanted to be a priest. He prayed that, if it be God's will, he would become one. He also prayed, through the intercession of Mary, whose litany he prayed every day after making his First Holy Communion, that he would become a bishop. Both prayers were answered. Throughout his life, Sheen believed that he was called to be another Christ, given as he said, his real autobiography, "was written twenty-one centuries ago, published and placarded in three languages, and made available to everyone in

---

[1] Sheen, *Those Mysterious Priests*, Doubleday & Co., Garden City, NY, 1974, p. 229. Appropriately enough, his last book was about the priesthood.

Western civilization." The mission given to the apostles was to go forth and preach and teach the Gospel to all nations. If ever there was a bishop who took these words to heart, it certainly is Fulton J. Sheen.

While yet a student, Sheen saw that the world was in difficulty. He believed man's problems were a result of man's indifference to his God and His plan for mankind. This was manifested with an anarchy of ideas and a breakdown of spiritual values. Difficulties could only be resolved by man's return to God. The return, like the return of the Prodigal son, though, would have to be on the Father's terms and not ours. Sheen addressed modern day errors not as problems but as opportunities and challenges. Though Sheen was referred to by G.K. Chesterton as "a product of the prevailing atmosphere of his times," Sheen was not intimidated by those times nor the personalities he encountered. Sheen could easily have been thwarted by those who did not adhere to his belief in the reality of a God who is present in all things and whose desire is that man live in a way consistent with His will. God's will was revealed to man with the coming of His Son and recounted for us in the Scriptures. Sheen believed it was his mission to advance the notion, to anyone willing to listen, that the Catholic faith, whose foundation is Jesus Christ, had solutions to the problems of the day. He engaged these problems using every modern day invention at his disposal whether in the classroom, pulpit, articles, books, radio or television.

While defining himself as a priest, Sheen could have been described also as a teacher. He loved teaching! For over twenty years he taught philosophy at Catholic University when he could easily have been in some other ministry. It was during those years that he sharpened his skills as a speaker and apologist. He believed that education, if it is to bear fruit, must be based on morality, religion and faith. He also believed that it was important for him to remain "relevant," or attentive to the questions of the day. Sheen maintained however that while he and the Church must stay relevant, he warned that those married to the age in which they live are soon widowed, stating that while the Church is always willing to take back *erring* souls into her treasury, she will not accept *errors* into the treasury of her wisdom. False prophets have always existed, even in the Church, proposing beliefs founded on half-truths and what the times will accept. Sheen insists that the Church...

> never suits the particular mood of any age, because it was made for all ages. A Catholic knows that if the Church married the mood of any age in which it lived, it would be a widow in the next age. The mark of the true Church is that it will never get on well with the passing mood of the world: "I have chosen you out of the world, therefore the world hates you" (Jn 15:19).[2]

Truth, Sheen taught, is not something we invent; if we do, it is a lie. Rather truth is something we discover.

> In contrast with the modern prophets, the message of Our Blessed Lord was not smart or sophisticated, but plain and simple. There is nowhere an attempt to impress His auditors either with His Omnipotence or with their nescience. He is never complex. There is no trick of rhetoric, no appeal to the intelligentsia, no pomp of demonstration, no monotonous deserts of laws and precepts such as are found in Buddha and Mohammed.[3]

---

[2] Sheen, *Love One Another*, p. 149.

[3] Sheen, *The Eternal Galilean*, p. 96.

The false prophets of the first half-century presented false truths which were accepted by many with the following result:

> The world had hoped for peace, and it got wars and rumors of wars; it was promised prosperity, and it got starvation in the midst of plenty; it had hoped to make the world safe for democracy, and got a democracy which was hardly safe for the world; it was promised a world free from authority and got tyrannical dictatorship. The result is that today instead of progress, evolution, prosperity, and World Peace, we have decay, unrest, uncertainty, doubt, and above all a feeling of not knowing where we are going.[4]

Sheen offered three suggestions for a return and preservation of the peace that man so desired but had not yet found. *First,* he believed that our prayer lives must shift from petition to reparation and intercession. Prayers of petition are good but it is in a crisis that we must ask favors for the entire world. *Second,* before attempting to change the world, we must begin to change *ourselves.* Sheen points out that Jesus came not to change the world but to change human hearts. He took twelve men apart from the world, purged their hearts, then gave them His Spirit, "*they* were changed, then *they* revolutionized the world." He believed that what the world needed were a few saints. He quotes Stalin who said, "It takes ten thousand men to build a bridge, it takes only two to destroy it." So too, "a few souls that are full of energy and the spirit of Christ can do more than thousands who are busybodies washing the outside of cups."[5] He protested that there were already too many who, like Peter,

---

[4] Sheen, *Philosophies at War*, New York, Scribner's, 1943, p. 326.

[5] Sheen, *On Being Human*, pp. 299-301. This book is an anthology of Sheen's writings.

would substitute action for prayer: "If the world is to rebuild from its foundations, then the way to make clean politics is to make good politicians; the way to have sound economics is to have moral economists." *Third*, a shift of emphasis from social justice to conversion of souls. Sheen does not negate the importance of social justice; indeed, he states that it must be pursued with "unrelenting energy," but we should realize that spiritual regeneration must precede social amelioration, that "social justice is an *effect* of moral living, and not its cause." He warns against those who have zeal but no truth and castigates those who have truth but no zeal. The approach to be followed is the one first suggested by Jesus, "Seek ye first the Kingdom of God and His Justice and all these things shall be added unto you."[6]

Sheen regretted that broad-mindedness had become the accepted norm rather than acknowledgment of truth.

> In order that the world might be made safe for so many conflicting points of view, broad-mindedness was cultivated as the most desirable of all virtues. The man who still believed in truth was often called narrow, while he who cared not to distinguish it from error was praised for his breadth.[7]

During the first half of this century, man fought two world wars and suffered through a depression. Sheen believed that all these were a product of the "Age of Reason" which he called an "Age of Unbelief." The philosophies of people like Kant, Hume and Voltaire were, in the words of Sheen, "corrosive." Their erroneous positions were such because they measured growth of reason by its alienation from God thus "the sover-

---

[6] *Ibid.*, passim.
[7] Sheen, *Freedom Under God* (New York: Bobbs-Merrill Co. 1947), p. 13.

eignty of reasonable people replaced the sovereignty of God."[8] Early on in life Sheen realized that there were those who were not interested in the truth as much as in being thought of as "novel," thus hoping to become famous. Sheen relates the story of a professor whose book Sheen had read and was disturbed by some of its conclusions. After some discussion of the book Sheen asked the professor a question: "I asked him if he would be interested in reading the philosophy of Saint Thomas Aquinas." "No, I would not be interested because you become known in this world not through Truth, but through novelty, and my doctrine is novel." So answered Dr. Alexander, of the University of Manchester in England who won an award from King George for his treatise on *Space, Time and Deity*. The thrust of his thesis was that God was evolving.[9]

It is the Church's role to continually remind man of the truth about his place in the cosmos. Man was created in the image and likeness of God *and* is subject to Him. God created man, not the other way around. Once man realizes and accepts this truth, he can both address and rise above life's difficulties and move on.

> Man alone, of all creatures, has a soul which is capable of knowing the infinite; he alone has aspirations beyond what he sees and touches and feels; he alone can attain everything in the world and still not be satisfied. That is why, when he misses the infinite and the eternal for which he was made and which alone can satisfy, he despairs.[10]

Christian truth, Sheen taught, can assist him. The death

---

[8] Sheen, *Philosophies at War*, p. 15.

[9] *TIC*, p. 25.

[10] *On Being Human*, p. 42.

knell of the Church has been rung many times through history but still she lives on, to the astonishment of philosophers, continuing to bring the message of the Gospel to the masses. Sheen is not surprised:

> The Church is not a continuous phenomenon through history. Rather, it is something that has been through a thousand resurrections after a thousand crucifixions. The bell is always sounding for its execution which, by some great power of God, is everlastingly postponed.[11]

Governments rise and fall, monarchs live and die, countries that once existed exist no more, but the Church continues, conveying the message of the Gospel which embodies the truth. Conversion, not condemnation, Sheen believed, had to be the Church's message. Sheen would make that message his own.

In addition to teaching at Catholic University, Sheen was active on the speaking circuit and the radio. The Catholic Hour began not only for the instruction of Catholics but all Americans. The radio was a medium used by Sheen for evangelization of Catholics about their faith, as well as informing others about Catholicism. There was a huge amount of misinformation about Catholics at the time and some would argue that there still is, much of which led to anti-Catholicism based upon not so much what people know but what they think they know: "Hatred comes from want of knowledge, as love comes from knowledge; thus bigotry is properly related to ignorance."[12] Sheen tells of receiving a letter from a man informing him that he had twelve books showing that the Pope was the Anti-Christ. The man was going to send them to Sheen after hearing him

---

[11] Sheen, *Three to Get Married*, (New York: Appleton-Century-Crofts, Inc., 1951), p. 221.

[12] *Way to Happiness*, p. 63.

speak about the Pope. However, Sheen kept referring in his talks to "the Holy Father" and "the Vicar of Christ." The man wrote to Sheen wondering when he would talk about the Pope, but also expressed an appreciation of what Sheen had to say about the Holy Father and Vicar of Christ![13]

Sheen used the radio to lessen bigotry of all kinds. Radio and the written word were the only sources of information for most people earlier in this century. Many listeners to the radio were non-Catholics interested in hearing about God from a man of God. Though not the first to use radio as a means of evangelization, Sheen's success led others to believe that they too could use the radio to transmit the Gospel. Wisely, Sheen learned from the debacles that ruined some of his peers to stay clear of politics and personalities. His stated purpose, and it bears repeating over and over again, was the salvation of souls. An unexpected but welcome result of his radio program was converts to the Catholic faith, in no small part due to his ability to make religion both plausible and appealing to people. Sheen realized that his success could very easily lead to a feeling of self-importance. He took to heart what he warned a young priest who told him he had already made seventy-two converts in six years of priesthood, namely, to stop counting, otherwise he might think that it was he who made them rather than God.

Though many of Sheen's books were scripted from his radio and television programs, Sheen had a talent for writing as well. Over a period of some sixty years, Sheen wrote sixty books. Many were bestsellers. While most of his books concerned religion, faith and God, many were written to answer the issues of the day. Three best sellers concerned the latest threats to man, namely the three ism's. From the vantage point of being a cleric, Sheen saw Fascism, Nazism and Communism

---

[13] *TIC*, p. 73.

as threats to the freedom his Church enjoyed, and to the freedom of every man, woman and child. Secularists, too, saw all three as threats to freedom but Sheen saw them as a threat because they were anti-God — the author of freedom. Not only societies and individuals were threatened, but also man's fundamental right to *believe*. Fascism, Nazism and Communism were not strong in and of themselves... it was only that Western Civilization had become weak. While many believed that answers to these problems were to be found in diplomacy and, if need be, war, Sheen believed that if we were to really win, victory and lasting peace would only come about as a result of a return to God and a renewal of the Christian spirit. While believing that war was a necessary evil, war could not be an end in itself.

Each of the ism's was a threat to the rights of man who was endowed with these rights by his Creator. Sheen correctly warned that Communism was the greatest threat. While Fascism and Nazism were a threat for a time (and could be again), thwarting Communism became Sheen's obsession. He warned that these threats were symptoms of a disease that had engulfed mankind. Ignorance and/or non-adherence to the will of God resulted in man's inhumanity to man. In light of the Gospel, man failed to realize that the tenets of the Gospel gave man both direction and meaning. Sheen primarily believed the threat to the world would be from Russia, not only because of her government and expansionist policies, but because the Blessed Virgin Mary had said so at Fatima. History shows that Sheen was correct concerning the threat from Communism and Russia. Russia was indeed a great threat to freedom for over seventy years and, as Mary warned, Russia did seek to spread her errors worldwide. Whether Russia would return to Christianity, as Sheen believed, remains to be seen, but Russia now, however precariously, enjoys freedoms that make that a possibility.

Whether the threat from Communism, as well as from other ism's has been removed is still in doubt. What is not in doubt is that society does not so much tacitly doubt the existence of God as much as it acts as if He doesn't exist. Sheen refers to this as the "Heresy of Action." Secular Humanism, as Sheen defines it, is Christianity without Christ, godliness without God, and Christian hope without the promise of eternal life. It seeks the exclusion of God from the day-to-day existence of people and is a threat that society has yet to fully appreciate.[14] Sheen asserts that it is a paradox that the same people who disparage religion have made a religion of Secular Humanism or what he refers to as "irreligious humanity." Perhaps the adage that "Christianity has not failed, it just hasn't been tried" is truer today than when first stated? Nonetheless, Sheen points out that Christianity has a "theology of the soul" to offer to humanity.

> Unless souls are saved, nothing is saved; there can be no world peace unless there is soul peace. World wars are only projections of the conflicts waged inside the souls of modern men; for nothing happens in the external world that has not first happened within a soul.[15]

Sheen's warning that unless there is first "soul peace" before there can be world peace is hard to argue with. One has only to look to our schools where disturbed young souls "act out" inner conflicts that are symptomatic of interior disorder. The lessons of the first half century have yet to be incarnated into our laws and consciences. The indifference to God and irreligion prior to two world wars is still prevalent today —

---

[14] *Old Errors and New Labels*, p. 215.
[15] *Peace of Soul*, p. 1.

even more so as evidenced with the lessening of respect for human life. Man was not ready to see that wars were the result of man's not being at peace with himself principally because he was not at peace with his God. Wars, which have always plagued mankind, continue because man refuses to deal with his own frailties which are rooted in an irreligious attitude. How had we gotten to this point, many wondered aloud during the two wars. Sheen said pointedly that one had only to look to the past to find out why. If man were truly serious about finding a cure for his ills, he had only to look to God.

Sheen, through the written word, as well as the airwaves, sought not only to educate about those dangers but how those dangers came to be and how to resolve them. America's past, founded on democratic ideals, was based upon a belief in God upon Whom it depended and under whose providence it continued to exist. Though a less than perfect society, America was still viewed as the one place in all the world where man could experience those rights given to him by God. America, though she had much to answer for, could still, if "righted" continue to be a refuge and beacon for the world. The separation of Church and State was instituted to protect the Church or Churches from the State and not the other way around. The Church, Sheen believed, could help America realize its potential for good.

Sheen was seen by many, at a time of great uncertainty, as reassuring and reasonable. A certain "reasonableness" was found in his expression, "Love the Communist, hate Communism," an expression based upon the teachings of Christ, namely, "Love the sinner, hate the sin." The only agenda that Sheen had was the salvation of souls. This came across to readers and viewers and was key to his popularity. His popularity as a spokesman for Catholicism and freedom on the American scene was unprecedented during these turbulent years. Over

the span of three decades, Sheen made an immeasurable contribution to the debate concerning threats to democracy and the
faith. His prominence as a spokesman against Communism was
an exceptional achievement in that he helped educate the nation, Catholic and non-Catholic about its dangers. The numerous awards he received from secular organizations are a testimony to the belief that in serving his Church, he had also served
his country and the world, all the time dispelling suspicions
about Catholics as well. As a result of the role the Church played
during the war and its position on Communism, "American
Catholics were no longer aliens and outcasts in America."[16] It
was Sheen, as American Catholicism's chief spokesman, who
helped bring this about.

The advent of television gave Sheen a new forum to make
the case for God. As he said in jest, he went on television to
assist his sponsor — the Lord. One can only conclude from his
success that he indeed did assist his sponsor. Others, during
his time had tried to imitate Sheen's success as a televangelist,
including Billy Graham, who had a short lived series in 1951
called *Hour of Decision*. But none came close to the popularity
and longevity of the "Microphone of God." Though Sheen received an Emmy in 1952 as the "Most Outstanding Personality Of The Year" (defeating Lucille Ball, Jimmy Durante, Edward R. Murrow, and Arthur Godfrey), he did not consider
himself a "personality." Concerning celebrity, Sheen noted that,
"anyone who steps into a shower, where he cannot carry his
press clippings, knows that his celebrity has not elevated him
above other men."[17] He recounts meeting a taxi driver who said
he watched him on television. He asked Sheen if he had ever
written a book. Sheen told him that he had, to which the driver

---

[16] Will Herberg, "A Jew Looks at Catholics," *Commonweal*, May 22, 1953, p. 177.
[17] *Way to Happiness*, p. 107.

replied: "If I didn't already have a book, I'd buy yours."

While he was the first religious communicator to have a sponsor for a program in prime time, Sheen did not like to think of himself as a television celebrity, as evidenced by the few pages he devoted to television in his autobiography. Rather, he saw himself fulfilling the mandate that was given him when ordained a priest — the spread of the Gospel. It would be in the television studio, though, that Sheen exhibited his teaching skills for all the world to see, skills that had made his classes at Catholic University standing room only. His only prop in the studio was a blackboard on which he wrote words or drew pictures that were effectual when trying to make a point. Whether he liked it or not, Sheen *was* a celebrity who received thousands of letters every day, was the most sought-after speaker in the country, and whose television show was watched by millions every week. As with the popularity of his books, when commenting on his popularity on television, Sheen maintained that popularity was not a concern. He felt repaid if he brought one person, one soul, closer to God, noting that "The Lord does not hold in great esteem those who are high in popularity polls: 'Woe to you when all men speak well of you.'"[18]

Sheen's concern for souls was not limited to those of the Catholic faith. He realized from the letters he received and viewers who watched his program, that many non-Catholics were responsive to what he had to say, proof that troubled souls know no denomination, race or color. As stated earlier, peace, which is the hope of every man, could not be realized unless one made peace with God. One also had to be at peace with his brother and sister regardless of race, creed or color. Sheen had an unparalleled opportunity to bring about mutual understanding between people using every medium available to him.

---

[18] *TIC*, p. 5.

Whether in print, on radio or television, he sought to make new friends for the Church and bring people with differing views together. He believed that this was doing the work of God: it was one of the final prayers of Christ on earth that we all might be one (Jn 17:21). Oneness, in a search and desire for truth.

> Today, there is a famine for divine certainty and guidance among those who spent the capital of their belief in Sacred Scripture; there is a famine for a helping hand more kindly than the human among those who spent belief in His Divinity; there is a famine for perfect life, truth, and love among those who spent belief in the Trinity. Everywhere there is a famine for faith among those who doubt, a famine for God among those who substituted illusions for majestic faiths, and a famine for love amongst those who war. Everywhere there is a feeling of emptiness like that which follows a fever or an unhappy love affair.[19]

Fulton Sheen was tailor-made to be bishop and head the Propagation of the Faith. As he tried to bring people with different beliefs together in his own country, he would have the opportunity to use his talents on a worldwide scale. His presence on television and the radio made him a household name on one continent and widely known in others. Many had gotten to know the name, if not the man. His ability to raise monies for different charities would now reach its zenith as head of the Propagation of the Faith. While his ability to raise money to meet the needs of the poor throughout the world was unsurpassed, his ability to enlighten souls in missionary territory was also first-rate. What he brought to people throughout the

---

[19] *The Prodigal World*, p. 16.

world was the Good News of hope… that there is something more. In doing so, he brought them hope for the future. While it was always his mission to bring Christ to people, he realized that those who as yet had not accepted Christ could *be* Christ both to and for others. He, like all Christians, would have to set the example. His three rules for dealing with converts would be used in handling those who differed from him religiously and culturally; as stated earlier they are: Kindness, kindness, kindness! His years in the missions not only affected others — he too was changed. He admitted that he realized as never before that the Gospel of Love, while being translated into different languages had to be translated into action on the part of the deliverers of the Gospel. "The Microphone of God" became the microphone for the poor and forsaken in the Church and society. His writings and television scripts spoke not so much about poverty as about the *poor*, not so much about hunger as the *hungry*, not so much about alienation as about those *alienated*, not so much about goods but *goodness*. The mediums that he used to make the Author of Spiritual Works of Mercy better known now also made better known the Corporal Works of Mercy. As once missionaries landed on the shores of Western Civilization and introduced the Gospel and with it freedom and prosperity, so now Sheen saw distant lands as modern day opportunities for evangelization. He believed that the more fortunate had a duty to assist others as dictated by the Gospel and in doing so they assist in their own salvation. Simply put, Love of God translated into love of neighbor.

> It is one of the paradoxes of Christianity that the only things that are really our own when we die is what we gave away in His name. What we leave in our wills is snatched from us by death; but what we give away is recorded by God to our eternal credit, for only our

works follow us. It is not *what* is given that profits unto salvation; it is *why* it is given.[20]

The Episcopacy that Sheen had prayed for and received enabled him, from a position of authority in the Church, to do much good for the poor. Though only five feet eight inches tall, Sheen appeared larger than life with his bishop's pectoral cross, zucchetto (skullcap), and crimson feriola (cape). His dress and appearance, as well as his words gave his audience a feeling of awe and reverence and helped Sheen to raise millions for those in need. This feeling enhanced his ability to speak with authority as a successor to the Apostles.

Sheen once stated that it was his desire that one day he might serve as an Ordinary of a diocese. That desire was granted by Pope Paul VI. While some said at the outset that the appointment was a mistake and a misuse of his talents, Sheen himself never said as much. Though he was not long an Ordinary of a diocese, the time he had was time enough for him to pave the way for others to implement the decrees of the Second Vatican Council. It has been said that only Richard Nixon could reach out to Communists given his reputation as an anti-Communist. Likewise, only Bishop Sheen, long described as a Traditionalist and friend of Popes, could be the first to establish relations with those of other faiths. His lifetime concern for the poor continued as Ordinary, challenging those in his diocese to do what they could to alleviate the sufferings of others.

Sheen's "preferential option for the poor" led to a decision made in haste that precipitated in his leaving Rochester. While one can legitimately criticize Sheen's method in "The St. Bridget's Affair," as many have, one cannot impugn his intention. Sheen saw a need and tried to meet it. One can look back

---

[20] *The Seven Virtues*, Garden City, NY, 1953, pp. 72-73.

on the whole episode and see that the damage done and hurt inflicted, chiefly concerned one individual — Sheen himself. At first, he was disillusioned by what happened but later accepted it as coming from God. Every suffering that one experiences is seen by Sheen as a purification by God. As he stated:

> My life, as I see it, is crossed up with the Crucifix. Only the two of us — my Lord and I — read it, and as the years go on we spend more and more time reading it together. What it contains will be telecast to the world on the Day of Judgment.[21]

Sheen always believed that God puts the illusions we have in life at the beginning in order that might come to know the real purpose of life as we get closer to eternity.

As a priest, Sheen believed that he was *victim* as well. Many would consider Sheen's book, *Life of Christ*, as his greatest. In his preface to the book, he states that for about ten years in his life he endured a great trial.[22] He claimed that he wrote the book to find solace in the Cross of Christ. He did not feel that the substance of that trial was important but expressed the feeling that those days were the most blessed days of his life. What was important, Sheen points out, was how the trial was met. He insists that it is not what happens to us that matters but how we react to it *and* that we offer it in union with the Cross... everything and every incident in our lives speak of God's love.

---

[21] *TIC*, p. 3.

[22] *Life of Christ* was first published in 1958 and republished in 1977. The preface in the newer version was written by Sheen at the time of its release. Sheen states that he wrote this book: "During those days when my life was backed up against the Cross, I began to know and to love it (the Cross) more. Out of it came this book. The point I sought to stress most clearly and more strongly was that the shadow of the Cross fell over every detail of the Life of Christ from the beginning" (p. 10).

The present moment includes some things over which we have control, but it also carries with it difficulties we cannot avoid — such things as a business failure, a bad cold, rain on picnic days, an unwelcome visitor, a fallen cake, a buzzer that doesn't work, a fly in the milk, and a boil on the nose the night of the dance. We do not always know why such things as sickness and setbacks happen to us, for our minds are far too puny to grasp God's plan. Man is a little like a mouse in a piano, which cannot understand why it must be disturbed by some one playing Chopin and forcing it to move off the piano wires. The things that happen to us are not always susceptible to our minds' comprehension or wills' conquering, but they are always within the capacity of our faith to accept and of our wills' submission. We would all like to make our own crosses; but since Our Lord did not make His own, neither do we make ours. We can take whatever He gives us and make the supernatural best of it.[23]

Sheen made use of his suffering in the same way that he used his talents. Both brought him to an awareness of the importance and presence of God. It has been said that the greatest tragedy in life is not becoming a saint. Sheen explains.

The great tragedy of history is not that men should fall, but that they should fail to rise to full realization of their vocation as children of God, in other words, that they should miss so much. Living second-rate, superficial, unimportant and morally insignificant lives, because they have never had their nature enkindled into flame by the Spirit of Christ.[24]

---

[23] *Lift Up Your Heart*, Doubleday & Company, Inc., Garden City, NY, 1950, pp. 202, 212-213.

[24] *The Mystical Body of Christ* (New York: Sheed and Ward, 1935), p. 258.

Though Sheen's last years entailed much physical suffering he continued to give talks around the country. He gave some forty-two lectures at universities between 1974 and 1977 until open-heart surgery in 1979 and a life of service took its toll. Shortly after his surgery, Sheen was asked to give an address at a National Prayer Breakfast. He agreed and brought his cardiologist with him. Billy Graham was in attendance and was asked to standby if Sheen could not finish. Graham recalls the event:

> President Carter was the President at the time. He (Sheen) looked very weak and tired and wan. However, when he stood up, the power of the Lord came upon him as I have seldom seen it come upon any man. He spoke with such conviction and authority — even turning to the President and Mrs. Carter and stating in effect: "You both are sinners and need redemption." This was one of the straightest evangelical messages I have ever heard given at one of the National Prayer Breakfasts. His eyes flashed, and he was the old Fulton Sheen that we had known so long on television.[25]

Sheen also wrote and gave interviews. Less than two years before his death he expressed a concern that while there had been much good in the Church as a result of the Second Vatican Council, spirituality had lessened. The tumult of the sixties and seventies had exacted a toll not only on society but in the Church as well. Sheen believed that concern for an individual soul had been replaced by an inordinate concern for society at the expense of the person. Quoting Mother Teresa, he believed that "concern for the poor without a love for Christ crucified is social work." Priests and religious are called to do

---

[25] George J. Marlin, *The Quotable Fulton Sheen*, Doubleday, New York, 1989, pp. 355-356.

more than just address the physical needs of the poor. Without this awareness, an inner conflict for many priests and religious arose which resulted in many of them leaving and empty seminaries.

> Today, salvation has become almost social. Many feel that if they carry the banner for social justice they need not be concerned about their personal morality. They become like David, who waxed angry when Nathan presented him with a social problem but whose conscience was not troubled about his own adultery. Both these extremes are wrong. Some in the Church may want to be on the mountain, isolated from the problems of the world such as the distraught father and his demonic son, while others struggle unsuccessfully with the later, because they have ceased to be prayerful. The two have to go together. The task of the Church in the years to come will be to unite the ecstasy and the valley. Without the mountain we have no vision, and without the valley our work is a heavy and leaden duty.[26]

As he so often does, Sheen refers back to the Scriptures in search of a remedy.

> The proper balance is found… in the story of Martha and Mary which follows in the Gospel the story of the Good Samaritan. In the latter, social service is praised. But in the story of Martha and Mary, it is suggested that we are not to become too absorbed in serving, that we have no time to sit at the feet of Jesus and learn His lessons.[27]

---

[26] David Kucharsky, "Bottom-Line Theology: An Interview with Fulton J. Sheen," *Christianity Today* 21, June 3, 1977, p. 9.

[27] *Those Mysterious Priests*, p. 20.

As mentioned earlier, Sheen believed that man had gone through several phases in the last few centuries: the Age of Faith, the Age of Reason, the Age of Unbelief. We now live in what Sheen calls "the Age of the Sensate." Doing what one feels is the way to go. Norms that were once based on Natural Law and the Scriptures have been abandoned. Philosophy, where ethics and morals were expressed and debated in colleges and universities, is no longer taught. What Sheen believes *is* taught is a kind of history of philosophy to which Sheen laments: "If we taught architecture today the way we teach philosophy, no one would ever be able to construct a building." In the Age of the Sensate, people do what they feel. Simply put, "My will be done," has been substituted for "Thy will be done." As long as it feels good, it is good. But what often feels good is sometimes contrary to the Law of God. What is contrary to the Law of God is rarely depicted as such and is usually explained or excused away. Sheen warns that, "It has always been the characteristic of a generation in decay to paint the gates of hell with the gold of paradise."[28]

Sheen did not live to see the consequences of the Age of the Sensate. As he believed that man's indifference to God led to two world wars and that a contraceptive mentality would lead to violence on an unprecedented scale, he was convinced that if man did not worship God, he would soon worship himself. This would be manifested with a concern about love replaced with an inordinate concern with sex.

> Sex divorced from love, instead of raising man by taking him away from himself, drags him down the hall of mirrors where he is always confronted with self. Sex does not care about the person, but about the act. The

---

[28] *The Moral Universe*, p. 108.

fig leaf that was once put over the secret parts of man and woman in sculpture is now put over the face. The person does not matter. The Victorians pretended it did not exist; the moderns pretend that nothing else exists.[29]

Pope Pius XII, is quoted as having said that "the greatest sin of the twentieth century is that it had lost all sense of sin." One has only to look at the lines for confession in our churches to see that this is true. Sheen believes that sin is not the worst thing in the world; the worst thing is the *denial* of sin. Sin is no longer personal but social. Everyone now is what Sheen calls "immaculately conceived." While there are many dangers that modern man faces, Sheen believes the gravest danger to moderns is the denial of sin.

The greatest danger facing modern society, one which has brought about the ruin of older civilizations and is destined to effect the collapse of our own unless we prevent it is the loss of the sense of sin.... There is the general denial that anything is wrong or that anything is right, and a general affirmation that what the older theological generation called "sin" is only a psychic evil or a fall in the evolutionary process.[30]

The loss of a sense of sin is of great concern to Sheen because he is concerned about souls and because of the effect sin has on one's faith.

In many cases those who lost the faith never did so for a *reason*. They left for a *thing*. Souls do not generally fall away because of the Creed; they first have difficulty

---

[29] *Those Mysterious Priests*, p. 314; also, *Peace of Soul*, p. 137.
[30] *The Hymn of the Conquered*, p. 72.

with the Commandments. The Creed, later on, becomes the handy tool of their rationalization: "I no
longer believe in Confession."[31]

The happiness that one receives from things in the world
is temporary and soon dissipated; one then feels impoverished
again. One has only to look at the shelves in our bookstores
which are filled with books about how to "achieve" happiness.
Sheen, like the great St. Augustine, observes that happiness is
not to be found in anything the world has to offer but only in
God.

> Man alone, of all creatures, has a soul which is capable
> of knowing the infinite, he alone has aspirations be-
> yond what he sees and touches and feels; he alone can
> attain everything in the world and still not be satisfied.
> That is why, when he misses the infinite and the eter-
> nal for which he was made and which alone can sat-
> isfy, he despairs.[32]

The despair that Sheen refers to is a given in today's society. Such "despair" is evidenced particularly among the young.
Violence, substance abuse and suicide have reached unparalleled proportions. A teacher from four decades ago and one
teaching today can see the dramatic change in the number and
kind of problems with which our youth are confronted.[33] The

---

[31] *Those Mysterious Priests*, p. 76.

[32] *On Being Human*, p. 42.

[33] "In the 1940's a survey listed the top seven discipline problems reported in public schools: talking, chewing gum, making noise, running in the halls, getting out
of turn in line, wearing improper clothes, and not putting paper in wastepaper
baskets. A 1980's survey lists these top seven: drug abuse, alcohol abuse, preg-
nancy, suicide, rape, robbery, assault. (Arson, gang warfare, and venereal disease
are also-rans.)" George Will quoted in *And I Quote, The Essential Public Speaking
Resource*, ed., Ashton Applewhite, St. Martin's Press, 1992, p. 330.

root of the problem is not social but personal. Many grow up not knowing the true God, thus they become attracted to false gods, celebrities and personalities and a kind of irreligion.

> The enthusiasm for false gods cannot be drowned by an indifference to the true God. No secularized, non-religious theory of political freedom is strong enough to overcome them. A people who lack the strength of an ultimate conviction, cannot overcome their faith or their false absolute. The effective answer to a false religion is not indifference to all religion, but the practice of a true religion. Their totalitarian, false religion can be overcome only by a total true religion.[34]

In speaking engagements at universities around the country, Sheen found his young audience receptive to the idea of sacrifice. He found that the more he spoke of the cross and sacrifice, the more they listened.

> Youth today has a potential for sacrifice that has not been tapped. The appeal of Nazism, Fascism, and Communism was to youth on the basis of dedication, consecration, and sacrifice to a race, a state or a party. It would almost seem as if dictators had snatched the crucifix from our hands, torn the Christ from it, held it aloft, and said to youth: "Take up your cross daily and follow the dictator." Too often, we have, on the contrary, taken the Christ without his cross, a Redeemer without his means of redemption, a Teacher to be equated with Buddha, Confucius, Tao.[35]

---

[34] *Philosophies at War*, op. cit., p. 168.

[35] *Missions and the World Crisis*, (Milwaukee, WI: The Bruce Publishing Co., 1963), p. 145.

The Christian, Sheen notes, has been enlightened by Christ and confronts the world as it is and not as we would like. The young, and adults for that matter, are looking for examples to follow, people whose lives are consistent with their beliefs. "Few of the boys who wanted to be Joe Namath five years ago want to be Joe Namath today. When touchdowns stop, imitation stops. As we cease to reflect Christ, the desire to be Christ declines."[36] Examples and answers can come from believers in the True God, but all too often their light, and this Jesus warns against, is kept under a bushel basket (Mt 5:14-16). Sheen issues a challenge and warning to those who bear the title "Christian."

> The torch of faith has been given to us not to delight our eyes but to enkindle the torches of our fellow men. Unless we burn and are on fire for the Divine Cause a glacial invasion will sweep the earth which will be the end, for "The Son of Man, when he cometh, shall he find, think you, faith on earth."[37]

Fear of persecution or alienation inhibit many from doing their Christian duty. Sheen believes that, unlike centuries ago, when the Church was persecuted or rejected because of her doctrines or beliefs, what the Church proposes today is rejected because of lifestyles or the "Heresy of Action."

> Minds no longer object to the Church because of the way they *think,* but because of the way they *live.* They no longer have difficulties with the Creed, but with her Commandments; they remain outside her saving wa-

---

[36] David Kucharsky, "Bottom-Line Theology: An Interview with Fulton J. Sheen," *Christianity Today* 21, June 3, 1977, p. 11.

[37] *The Rainbow of Sorrow,* (New York: P.J. Kenedy and Sons, 1938), p. 71.

ters, not because they cannot accept the doctrines of the Three Persons in One God, but because they cannot accept the moral of two persons in one flesh; not because Infallibility is too complex, but because the veto on Birth Control is too hard; not because the Eucharist is too sublime, but because Penance is too exacting. Briefly, the heresy of our day is not the heresy of thought, it is the heresy of action.[38]

The Christian must be careful not to become so complacent or indifferent to what is going on around him that he loses sight of the goal.

Those who lose sight of the goal often concentrate on mere motion and try to derive pleasure from it. They delight in turning the pages of a book, but never finish the story; they pick up brushes, but never finish a picture; they travel the seas, but know no ports. Their zest is not in the achievement of a destiny but rather in gyration and action for the mere sake of movement.[39]

While Sheen bemoans the state that society finds itself in today, he insists that because man, in the silence of his heart seeks the good, a spiritual awakening in the world can still take place.

…it is still true that the twentieth century is closer to God than the nineteenth century was. We are living on the eve of one of the great spiritual revivals of human history. Souls are sometimes closer to God when they feel themselves farthest away from Him, at the point of despair.[40]

---

[38] *Communism and the Conscience of the West,* pp. 142-143.
[39] *Way to Happiness,* p. 163.
[40] *On Being Human,* p. 86.

He wants those who have fallen away from their faith, for whatever reason, to realize that:

> *Modernized, the Easter message means that God recycles human garbage.* He can turn prostitutes like Magdalen into disciples, broken reeds like Simon Peter into rocks, and political-minded Simon Zealots into martyrs for the faith. *God is the God of the Second Chance.*[41]

In its totality, the life and ministry of Archbishop Fulton J. Sheen was about saving souls. He believed that the only way to win people was preaching Christ crucified. When He spoke of suffering and sacrifice, he realized that some would turn away, but they turned away from the Lord as well. Sheen's *raison d'être* was not surprising for it was in keeping with his role as a priest.

Many have asked about the secret of Sheen's success. He always responded firmly that it was the Holy Hour. In the presence of the Lord he received his inspiration. When people asked him how they were to become holy, Sheen simply responded: "Get down on your knees, for it is the language of the saints." Sheen spent many an hour on his knees. Perhaps many more hours on his knees especially when he tasted failure for the first time as bishop of Rochester. He was able to put that "dolor" or suffering behind him to attend to the needs of the Church for the remaining years given him. Sheen's life took many different directions, and yet he was able to adapt to the different times. Though he did not like to be thought of as "Traditional," his life demonstrates that he could be described as orthodox doctrinally, and progressive socially, who used what, at the time, were considered unorthodox methods.

---

[41] *Those Mysterious Priests*, p. 126.

During his years at Catholic University, Sheen had to decide what route he would take: remaining a scholar and philosopher, far removed from most of the masses, or a popularizer of the faith. To the criticism made against him that he was never really part of the intelligentsia but was simply a very bright and gifted performer, Sheen would wholeheartedly agree, with one qualification: not a part of the intelligentsia, but truly an intellectual.

> The intellectual never loses that compassion for the multitude which characterized the Word Incarnate. The intelligentsia, on the contrary live apart from tears and hunger, cancer and bereavements, poverty and ignorance. They lack the common touch. Only the cream of bookish learning and not the milk of human kindness flows through their veins. The true intellectual is never separated from the masses. The Word became Flesh and talked in parables. If we are truly intellectual, we have to be able to give examples of what we know. We never understand anything until we give an example. I have not been among the intelligentsia, but I have been an intellectual.[42]

Sheen certainly did not lack the common touch. Monsignor John Tracy Ellis worked for Sheen for a time as his secretary, and lived with him in the 1930's. Until his death, this dean of American Catholic scholars believed that "the contribution of Fulton Sheen to the Catholic Church and the general American public was incalculable,"[43] and "anyone who would deny the fact of his contribution being a great one is either unfair or

---

[42] *The Priest Is Not His Own,* McGraw Hill, New York, 1963, p. 22.

[43] John Tracy Ellis, *Catholic Bishops: A Memoir*, Michael Glazier, Inc., Wilmington, DE, 1983, p. 83. Ellis found Sheen "an all together agreeable employer. He was unfailingly kind and generous during the time I served him as secretary" (p. 79).

does not know of what he speaks."[44] But Monsignor Ellis also believed that Sheen had a serious flaw — his vanity.

> He was a steady worker, devoted to the daily Mass, and I witnessed his legendary long hours. They were no myth. He made sure to have two priests living with him so that the Eucharist could be present. But he had one serious flaw — his vanity. That was a little tedious. He was a very vain man, but that's not the worst of faults and there is a distinction between vanity and pride.[45]

For fifty years, Sheen touched the minds and hearts of his readers and listeners. That "touch" did not end with his death. In doing the research and writing of this book, I have encountered many people who remember Bishop Sheen. Many remember hearing him on the radio. Others recall how they would look forward all day to seeing him on television in the evening. Many remember hearing him preach in the great cathedrals and in small country churches. Many recalled the effect that he had on their lives and their relationship to God. While a seminarian at St. Joseph's Seminary, I brought up Sheen in class and noted the effect he had on both the local and universal Church. The professor replied that while Sheen was suitable for his time, he no longer was of any real relevance and was in fact dated. What he didn't know was that many of his students were reading Sheen's works. Many had his books in their private libraries. I cannot number the times a person responded "Oh, I loved

---

[44] Kathleen Riley Fields, "Fulton J. Sheen: An American Catholic Response to the Twentieth Century," dissertation, Notre Dame University, South Bend, IN, 1989. From an interview by author with Monsignor John Tracy Ellis on February 20, 1987. See p. 596.

[45] James Breig, "And Now A Word With Our Sponsor," *U.S. Catholic*, February 1980, p. 26.

him," or, "Oh, he was just great" when I mentioned his name. Only recently, twenty years after Sheen's death, a young woman was telling me that she had not long ago watched a video of one of his programs and she mentioned how much it had moved her. She wished that she could hear him talk in person. When I replied that it would be impossible, she asked me why, to which I replied, "Well he's no longer with us." Startled, she replied, "I can't believe it, he seemed so much alive." As to greatness, William Hazlitt once said, "No man is truly great who is great only in his lifetime. The test of greatness is the page of history."

If Sheen were still with us, just beginning his ministry as a priest and teacher, would he still have the same immense appeal that he did in previous decades? It must be acknowledged that in the first half of this century, many threats to humanity were recognized and dealt with. The rights of man were threatened as never before. Defenders of God and liberty were given a platform because the times demanded it. People needed to be reassured that there was a God in whom they could place their trust, that all would turn out well. Communism, Nazism and Fascism held a strange fascination for many and perhaps these threats would have had many more supporters had there not been a Fulton Sheen on the scene. The mediums of radio and television were fresh and new. There weren't many choices. Today, there are many choices of what we will watch or listen to, including an explosion of available programs on cable television. Some of this has been good, but much of it unsavory and harmful, corrupting minds of young and old alike, appealing to the lower impulses of man and woman. Much of it is monotonous. A recent popular song claims as much, exclaiming that there are fifty seven channels with nothing on, and yet… their audience grows. Sheen's weekly audience, it must be remembered numbered in the millions in the 1950's! Many of the most highly rated television programs today do not command the audience he did. Would a national sponsor and station be available for Sheen today, willing to put *Life is Worth Living*, or a program like it on at prime time? Would public service matter in the deliberations, or only ratings, which result in many programs not lasting long enough to even find an audience? Would there be an audience for a program about life based on man's relationship with his Creator and fellow man? Is there now or in the future someone who could match Sheen? Those are "what if" questions without an easy answer.

What we do know is that the times are far different from the times when Sheen's appeal reached its zenith. Today's stars are yesterday's news. Moderns do not only want to be enlightened but entertained. Institutions, based on authority, in both the Church and society, have nowhere near the influence they once did. Those same institutions have not yet recovered from the scandals of our present day. These scandals in our country, our government, and many churches, have made people more skeptical of their leaders and the institutions they represent, including religion. Role and authority have given way to charisma. Attendees at Mass on any given Sunday hear homilies that are devoted to the importance of loving one's neighbor but rare is the homily on loving one's God by fulfilling His precepts. Would today's permissive society be open to or feel threatened by hearing about "the heresies of action," namely, the evils of abortion, infidelity, divorce, unnatural sex and sex outside of marriage? Reality would require us to admit that in today's permissive society, many will have practiced one of the above and/or know someone who has. Is there a sincere desire on the part of people for the truth? With so many voices and different messages clogging the airwaves claiming to have the truth, how are people to discern the truth? Sheen cautioned that truth has a narrow path and that on either side is an abyss. He believed that it would be in the realm of ideas that the world would be restored.[46] To seek the truth, he reasoned, could be as thrilling as a romance.

> As a scientist can reveal to me the truths which are beyond my reason, so God can reveal to me truths which are beyond the power of my intelligence. Since I know Him to be One Who neither deceives nor can be deceived, so I accept His revelation in faith.[47]

Though there are many personalities in the Church who have achieved prominence and success within their religious circles, either through writing, on radio and/or television, there is no one yet who has reached the universal appeal of a Fulton Sheen. Indeed, anyone seeking Sheen's mantle would have to have an appeal that goes *outside* their particular environs. One thing remains constant however — the desire on the part of people to be reassured in an increasingly insecure world. Sheen succeeded because he helped many people of many different faiths and backgrounds believe that... *life is worth living.*

It has been some twenty years since his death, and many of his books are being republished, along with his tapes, and videos of his television show *Life is Worth Living*. His autobiography, *Treasure in Clay*, first published in 1980, was re-issued in 1993. His book *The World's First Love* (1952), a book on the Blessed Virgin Mary, was republished in 1996 and is considered a bestseller, and *Life is Worth Living* (1953) was republished in March of 1999.[48] Several books and dozens of articles have been

---

[46] *Seven Pillars of Peace*, p. 5.

[47] *Guide to Contentment*, (New York: Alba House, 1996), p. 110.

[48] In a phone interview with Christopher Veneklase, Operations Manager at Ignatius Press Publications, on October 1, 1999, Mr. Veneklase stated that "since 1993, the republished issue of *Treasure in Clay* has sold over 12,000 copies. Since 1996,

written about him and anthologies of his works are widely available. His books are widely available for purchase on the Internet.[49] His books on the priesthood are available in bookstores and used in seminaries around the world. It would seem that Sheen still has something to say concerning God, faith and freedom that continues to find an audience, testimony to the popularity, longevity and versatility of this man of God.

In the first few pages of this book, I used only half of a quotation from Sheen concerning his life and how he believes God will judge him. Here is the rest of what he had to say.

> ...there have been moments in that autobiography when my heart leapt for joy at being invited to His Last Supper; when I grieved when one of my own left His side to blister His lips with a kiss; when I tried falteringly to help carry His gibbet to the Hill of the Skull; when I moved a few steps closer to Mary to help draw the thrust sword from her heart; when I hoped to be now and then a disciple like the disciple called "Beloved"; when I rejoiced at bringing other Magdalenes to the Cross to become the love we fall just short of in all love; when I tried to emulate the centurion and press cold water to thirsty lips; when, like Peter, I ran to an empty tomb and at the seashore, had my heart broken a thousand times as He kept asking over and over again in my life: "Do you love Me?" These are the more edifying moments of the autobiography which can be

---

14,700 copies of *The World's First Love* have been purchased and since March of 1999, the month of its re-issue, 3,000 copies of *Life Is Worth Living* have been sold. Considering our market, Ignatius Press considers *The World's First Love* as a best seller while both *Treasure in Clay* and *Life Is Worth Living* are both selling very well."

[49] When I began my research for this book there were only about a dozen listings of books by Sheen or about him on a major Internet book seller list. As I write these pages, there are over sixty such listings.

written as a kind of second and less authentic edition than the real autobiography written two thousand years ago.[50]

Sheen believed that God will see his life in a different light, for: "Man reads the face but God reads the heart." How God will judge him he knew not but he believed that God would look upon him with mercy and compassion. He expected to be surprised by three things in Heaven: "First of all, I will see some people there I never expected to see. Second, there will be a number whom I expected to be there who will not be there. And, even relying on His mercy, the biggest surprise of all may be that I will be there."[51]

Sheen died in the presence of the Blessed Sacrament, on December 9th, 1979, one day after the Solemnity of the Immaculate Conception and only recently a day established by the Church as a memorial to Blessed Juan Diego, to whom Mary appeared in Guadalupe, Mexico, in 1531. Though making a Holy Hour was a personal practice, devotion to Mary was something that Sheen hoped every Christian would strive towards. Some of the last words of Christ on the Cross concerned His mother and her relationship to us. As she was at the side of her Son in the midst of his suffering, so too, the woman that we are blest to call "Mother," at the instruction of her Son, is at our side to offer consolation and reassurance to us as well, "now and at the hour of our death." Her openness to the will of God *caused* Mary to do great things. Sheen lived out his belief in the powerful presence and intercession of Mary in his life. His adherence to her directive as found in Scripture, "Do whatever He tells you," enabled him to do great things as well. He be-

---

[50] *TIC*, pp. 2-3.

[51] *Ibid.*, pp. 1, 2, 3, 6 respectively.

lieved that his devotion to Mary brought him to experience a new dimension to the sacredness of suffering. We can imagine that she was there at his side — as he believed she was all during his life — when Archbishop Fulton J. Sheen "shook off this earthly coil" and entered into the presence of the Lord whom he had served so faithfully. And he surely must have smiled as he heard Jesus say to him those words he had always longed to hear, "Enter in, for I've heard my mother speak of you."

Sheen's Reflections
On His 50th Anniversary As A Priest

"Sit down quickly and write me fifty." (Lk 16:6)

The twentieth day of September, nineteen sixty-nine,
Thanks to the mercies of the Good Lord,
I am a priest for fifty years.
No celebration marks the anniversary except your prayers
And my own silent thanksgiving in a Trappist Monastery.
And know why: any good done in these five decades
Was because God held my hand.
"What do you have that was not given to you?
And if it is given, how can you boast as if it were your own?"
    (1 Cor 5:7)
Only the worthless things are mine, when my ego walked
    alone.
If it be a terrible thing to fall into the hands of the Living
    God,
It is a more terrible thing to fall out of them.

IN RETROSPECT

In that scroll of years, for what am I most thankful?
— First, when born, my mother, like Hannah,
Laid me at the altar of the Blessed Mother
And dedicated me to the service of her Son.
This is my blessed assurance that the Lord will one day say:
"I heard My Mother speak of you."

161

— Second, that each morn at Holy Mass,
I could hear drifting from a Cross:
"Can you drink My cup?"
"Can you watch an hour?"
— Third, thanks, dear Lord, for suffering to see that not all
    crosses are on hills.
"Dragged like a plowshare through the heart,
only new furrows cause the grain to start."
— Fourth, as a bishop, I might as head feel the pain of every
member of his body.
And as a weak cell of that body, sense unity with brother
    priests
who love that head whose name is Peter.
— Fifth, my thanks to our *Presbyterium*,
for my brothers of Bread and Cup.
Who have met with me in shared griefs and joys
and daily restored the spiritual fortune of the diocese.
As "God restored Job's fortune because he prayed for his
    friends." (Job 42:10)

IN PROSPECT

What do I see and hope?
I see the Lord cleaning house,
testing the Church as He did the Germans with Nazism,
the Russians with Communism,
and us with worldliness and half-drawn blades.
I see the few who lose their way,
but thank God, because they never throw away the map,
and one day will come home again.
I see that if Secular Man turns us off,
it is because we gave him only paperback sociology,
and not the *Theology of the Crucified*.
The doubting Thomas, will believe only

when we show the red scars of love.
I see that we must dig holes
until we have something to build therein;
that if our scalpels are poisoned with hate,
we can bring no healing to broken wings.
That though some may tear at Mother Church's flesh,
yet not one bone of the Body will ever be broken.
I saw that fifty years ago we were wrong in saying:
"The Word became flesh and dwelt among us
Churchgoers, the respectable, the good and the white."
And I see that we are wrong today in changing the tune:
"The Word became flesh and dwelt among the Rebels,
the blacks and the protesters."
We will be right again when we believe God is the Father
        of all men,
and show Christ to the Negroes that they will see Him black,
and they will show Him to us, that we will see Him as white.
I see a rebirth of a priesthood
that will love the poor, without hating the rich,
that will serve the Church not despising those who bear its
        agonies,
and whose every dialogue will begin with a monologue
        before God.
I see the more we priests love, the more we will suffer,
as the distraught father suffers more than the delinquent son.
But our suffering love will take the worst this world can
        offer,
and press it as another drop in the chalice of Redemption.
I see that our gravity is too earthly — we are weighed with
        prayerless days.
Oh! To trust our weight on the Weightless Spirit,
and step out like astronauts on the shelf of grace,
and not fall, as Christ holds our hand.

CONCLUSION

My work, please the Lord, is not finished.
Much is still to be done, while there is light.
Non recuse laborem.
To close the generation gap,
each day I will say:
"I will go to the altar of God, to God who renews my youth."
The Lord did not begin to preach Wisdom and the Cross
until He was over thirty.
So I await His Promise to those planted in the House of God:
"They will bear fruit in old age,
still remaining fresh and green." (Ps 92:14)
As I work under the aegis of two hearts —
One Sacred and the other Immaculate,
I will sing with Hammarskjold:

> "The road,
> *I shall follow it.*
> The fun,
> *I shall forget it.*
> The cup,
> *I shall empty it.*
> The pain,
> *I shall conceal it.*
> The truth,
> *I shall be told it.*
> The end,
> *I shall endure it.*

Chronology

1895 - Born in El Paso, Illinois, the son of Newton Morris Sheen and Delia Fulton Sheen, May 8

1913 - Graduated from Spalding Institute (The Brothers of Mary) in Peoria, Illinois

1919 - Attended St. Viator's College and Seminary, Bourbonnais, Illinois. Attended St. Paul's Seminary, St. Paul, Minnesota

1919 - Ordained, September 20

1920 - S.T.F., J.C.B., Catholic University of America.

1923 - Attended the Sorbonne in Paris and Collegio Angelico in Rome

1926 - First American to receive the Cardinal Mercier Prize for International Philosophy (University of Louvain)

1930 - Began the Catholic Hour Broadcasts sponsored by the National Council of Catholic Men on the National Broadcasting Corporation Networks, 1930-1952

1934 - Appointed Papal Chamberlain by Pope Pius XII

1935 - Appointed Domestic Prelate by Pope Pius XII

1936 - Received the Cardinal Mazella Prize from Georgetown University

1940 - Speaker for the first religious service ever to be telecast

1950 - National Director of the Propagation of the Faith, 1950-1966

1951 - Appointed Bishop by Pope Pius XII. Auxiliary Bishop of New York 1951-1966

1952 - *Life is Worth Living*, television series begins, 1952-1957

1952 - Received television's "Emmy Award" and the "LOOK Television Award"

1952 - Became the first Latin Rite Bishop in history to offer a Solemn Byzantine Rite Mass in English

1953 - Received the Marian Library Award from the University of Dayton, Dayton, Ohio and the Cardinal Gibbons Award from the Alumni Association of the Catholic University of America for "distinguished and meritorious service to the Church, the United States and the Catholic University"

1959 - *The Bishop Sheen Program* television series

1960 - Consecrated missionary bishops with Pope John XXIII in St. Peter's, Rome, 1960 - May 1961

1962- *The Life of Christ* television series

1964 - *Quo Vadis America* television series

1964 - Received the Order of Lafayette Freedom Award for distinguished leadership in fighting Communism

1965 - Appointed to Vatican Council II Commission on the Missions by Pope Paul VI

1965 - Narrator for the Columbia Broadcasting System's coverage of Pope Paul's visit to the United Nations in New York City

1965 - *The Bishop Sheen Program* television series. His first television series to air in color

1966 - Appointed Bishop of Rochester, New York, by Pope Paul VI, 1966-1969

1966 - Elected by the American Episcopacy Chairman of the Committee for the Propagation of the Faith

1966 - Elected by the American Episcopacy to the Administrative Board of the National Council of Catholic Bishops

1969 - Appointed to the Papal Commission for Nonbelievers by Pope Paul VI

1969 - Named Archbishop of the Titular See of Newport (Wales) by Pope Paul VI

1976 - Named Assistant to the Pontifical Throne by Pope Paul VI

1979 - Meets in October with Pope John Paul II at St. Patrick's Cathedral on his first visit to the United States. After embracing Archbishop Sheen, the Holy Father tells him, "You have spoken and written well of the Lord Jesus and you are a loyal son of the Church."

1979 - Dies at his home on December 9th and is buried in the Crypt at St. Patrick's Cathedral

Degrees:

J.C.B., Catholic University of America, 1920
Ph.D., University of Louvain, Belgium, 1923
S.T.D., Rome, 1924
Agrégé en philosophie, Louvain, 1925
Honorary: LL.D, Litt. D., L.H.D.

Educator:

Dogmatic Theology professor, St. Edmund's College, Ware, England,
    1925
Philosophy professor, Catholic University of America, 1926-1950

Preacher:

Summer Conferences, Westminster, London, 1925, 1928, 1931
Catholic Summer School, Cambridge University, 1930-1931
Annual Broadcasts, *The Catholic Hour*, 1930-1952
Preacher at St. Patrick's Cathedral, New York City, 1930-1952

Editor:

World Mission and *Mission* magazines

Columnist:

"God Love You," Catholic Press
"Bishop Sheen Writes," Secular Press

Bibliography

A. Books by Fulton Sheen

The Church, Communism and Democracy (New York: Dell Publishing Co., 1964).

Communism and the Conscience of the West (Indianapolis and New York: Bobbs-Merrill Co., 1948).

The Cross and the Beatitudes (New York· P.J. Kenedy and Sons, 1937).

The Cross and the Crisis (Milwaukee: The Bruce Publishing Co., 1938).

The Divine Romance (New York: Alba House, 1996 and 1982; Garden City Books, 1950; originally published in 1930).

The Electronic Christian (New York: Macmillan Publishing Co., 1979).

The Eternal Galilean (New York: Alba House, 1997; Garden City Books, 1950; originally published in 1934).

God and Intelligence in Modern Philosophy (Garden City, NY: Doubleday and Co., 1958; originally published in 1925 by Longmans, Green and Co., London and New York).

God and War (New York: P.J. Kenedy and Sons, 1942).

God Love You (Garden City, NY: Doubleday and Co., 1955).

Go To Heaven (New York: The Dell Publishing Co., 1960; originally published in 1949).

Guide to Contentment (New York: Alba House, 1996).

Jesus, Son of Mary (Liguori, MO: Liguori Publications, 1995, originally published in 1948 by Declan X. McMullen Co.).

The Last Seven Words (New York: Alba House, 1995 and 1982; Garden City Books, 1952).

Liberty, Equality and Fraternity (New York: The Macmillan Co., 1938).

Life is Worth Living - Series 1-5 (New York: McGraw-Hill, 1953-57).

169

The Life of All Living (New York: Garden City Books, 1951; originally published in 1929).

Life of Christ (Garden City, NY: Image Books, 1977; New York: McGraw-Hill, 1958).

Lift Up Your Heart (New York: Garden City Books, 1952; originally published in 1950).

Love One Another (New York: Garden City Books, 1953; originally published in 1944).

Missions and the World Crisis (Milwaukee: The Bruce Publishing Co., 1963).

Moods and Truths (New York: Appleton-Century Co., 1934).

The Mystical Body of Christ (New York: Sheed and Ward, 1935).

Old Errors and New Labels (New York: The Century Co., 1931).

Peace of Soul (Liguori, MO: Liguori Publications, 1996; Garden City, New York: Doubleday and Co., 1954; originally published in 1949).

Philosophy of Religion (New York: Appleton-Century-Crofts, Inc., 1948).

Preface to Religion (New York: P.J. Kenedy and Sons, 1946).

The Priest Is Not His Own (London: The Catholic Book Club, 1963).

The Rainbow of Sorrow (New York: P.J. Kenedy and Sons, 1938).

Religion Without God (New York: Garden City Books, 1954; originally published in 1928).

Seven Last Words (New York: Alba House, 1995 and 1982).

That Tremendous Love (New York: Harper and Row, 1967).

Those Mysterious Priests (Garden City, New York: Doubleday and Co., 1974).

Three to Get Married (New York: Appleton-Century-Crofts, Inc., 1951).

Treasure in Clay: The Autobiography of Fulton J. Sheen (San Francisco, CA: Ignatius Press, 1993; Garden City, NY: Doubleday and Co., 1980).

The Way of the Cross (New York: Appleton-Century-Crofts, Inc., 1932).

Way to Happiness (New York: Alba House, 1997).

Way to Inner Peace (New York: Alba House, 1994; Garden City Books, 1955).

Whence Come Wars (New York: Sheed and Ward, 1940).

The World's First Love (San Francisco: Ignatius Press, 1996; originally published in 1952).

B. Articles by Fulton J. Sheen

"Assumption and the Modern World," *Thomist* 14 (January, 1951), 31-40.

"Bishop Fulton J. Sheen Tells the Story of the Birth of Christ," *Collier's* 132 (December 25, 1932), 23-27.

"Christ Was There First," *Worldmission* 17 (Summer, 1966), 3-17.

"The City and the World," *Worldmission* 15 (Summer, 1964), 3-11.

"The Coronation of Pope John XXIII," *Worldmission* 9 (Winter, 1958), 3-6.

"Do You Know What Communism Is," *Catholic Digest* 9 (July 1947), 76-81.

"How to Convert the Moslems," *Worldmission* 8 (Fall, 1957), 3-11.

"Mary and the Russians," *Our Lady's Digest* 10 (November, 1955), 163-166.

"Mercier and Thomism," *Commonweal* 3 (February 10, 1926), 372-373.

"Moscow Makes Confusion for Reds and for Nations," *America* 62 (October 28, 1939), 60-61.

"Soviet Russia May Be Helped, But Russia Must Be Reformed," *America* 66 (October 18, 1941), 33-35.

"Spain Through Red Tinted Glasses," *The Irish Monthly* 67 (March, 1939), 169-180.

C. Books and Pamphlets about Fulton Sheen

Conniff, James C.G., *The Bishop Sheen Story*, Greenwich, CT: Fawcett Publications Inc., 1953.

Lynch, Christopher Owen, *Selling Catholicism: Bishop Sheen and the Power of Television*, Kentucky: University Press of Kentucky, 1998.

Marlin, George J., *The Quotable Fulton Sheen*, New York: Doubleday, 1989.

Massa, Mark S., *Catholics and American Culture; Fulton Sheen, Dorothy Day, and the Notre Dame Football Team*, New York: Crossroad Publishing Company, 1999.

Noonan, Daniel P., *The Passion of Fulton Sheen*, New York: Dodd, Mead and Co., 1972.

D. Other Books

Abbott, Walter, S.J.(ed.), *The Documents of Vatican II*, London: Geoffrey Chapman, 1966.

Budenz, Louis Francis, *This is My Story*, New York: Whittlesey House, The McGraw-Hill Book Co., 1947.

Cohalan, Florence D., *A Popular History of the Archdiocese of New York*, New York: United States Catholic Historical Society, 1983.

Delaney, John J., *Dictionary of American Catholic Biography*, Garden City, NY: Doubleday, 1984.

Ellis, John Tracy, *American Catholicism*, 2nd ed., Chicago: University of Chicago Press, 1969.

_____, *Catholic Bishops: A Memoir*, Wilmington, DE: Michael Glazier, Inc., 1983.

Noonan, Hugh (ed.), *The Pastoral Letters of the American Hierarchy, 1792-1970*, Washington, DC: United States Catholic Conference, 1984.

Roche, Douglas J., *The Catholic Revolution*, New York: David McKay Co., 1968.

E. Articles about Fulton Sheen

Bates, Ernest Sutherland, "A Champion of Reason," *Commonweal* 3, January 13, 1926, 264- 265.

Breig, James, "Fulton J. Sheen: And Now A Word With His Sponsor," *U.S. Catholic* 45, February, 1980, 24-28.

Daly, John Jay, "The Man Behind the Mike," *Sign* 24, May 10, 1945, 509-512.

Herberg, Will, "A Jew Looks at Catholics," *Commonweal* 58, May 22, 1953, 174-177.

Kucharsky, David, "Bottom-Line Theology: An Interview with Fulton J. Sheen," *Christianity Today* 21, June 3, 1977, 8-11.

Palmer, Gretta J., "Bishop Sheen on Television," *Catholic Digest* 17, February 1953, 75-80.

_____, "Bishop Fulton J. Sheen," *Catholic Digest* 15, October 1951, 55-62.

Shine, Donald, S.J., "Bishop Sheen's Threshold Apologetics," *American Ecclesiastical Review* 125, October 1951, 254-259.

H. Unpublished Sources

Fields, Kathleen Riley, "Fulton J. Sheen: An American Catholic Response to the Twentieth Century," Ph.D. dissertation, Notre Dame University Press, South Bend, Indiana, 1989.

Finks, P. David, "Crisis in Smugtown: A Study of Conflict, Churches and Citizen Organizations in Rochester, New York, 1964-1969," Ph.D. dissertation, Union Graduate School of the Union for Experimental Colleges and Universities, 1975.

INDEX

A

175

This book was designed and published by St. Pauls/ Alba House, the publishing arm of the Society of St. Paul, an international religious congregation of priests and brothers dedicated to serving the Church through the communications media. For information regarding this and associated ministries of the Pauline Family of Congregations, write to the Vocation Director, Society of St. Paul, 7050 Pinehurst, Dearborn, Michigan 48126. Phone (313) 582-3798 or check our internet site, www.albahouse.org